QuickStudy®

for

French

BarCharts inc
publishing

Boca Raton, Florida

©2007 BarCharts, Inc.
ISBN 13: 9781423202714
ISBN 10: 1-4232-0271-6

BarCharts® and QuickStudy® are registered trademarks of BarCharts, Inc.

Author: Liliane Arnet
Publisher:
       BarCharts, Inc.
       6000 Park of Commerce Boulevard, Suite D
       Boca Raton, FL 33487
       www.quickstudy.com

Printed in Thailand

Contents

- Avoir *(to have)*
- Être *(to be)*
- Faire *(to do, to make)*
• Passive Voice
• Verbs to Remember

Study Hints

NOTE TO STUDENT:
Use this QuickStudy® booklet to make the most of
your studying time.

QuickStudy® notes provide need-to-know information; read them carefully to better understand key
concepts.

NOTES
Nouns are either feminine or masculine,
whether they refer to a person, place, thing,
quality or idea, and are usually accompanied
by an article.

QuickStudy® examples offer detailed explanations;
refer to them often to avoid problems.

Examples:
- **C'est ma mère ici** *(It's my mother here).*
- **Où est la tienne?** *(Where is yours?)*

**Take your learning to the next level
with QuickStudy®!**

Abbreviations

Here is a key to abbreviations used throughout this book:

(fam.)	=	familiar/informal
(form.)	=	formal/polite
(masc.) / (m.)	=	masculine
(fem.) / (f.)	=	feminine
(sing.)	=	singular
(pl.)	=	plural

Pronunciation & Rules of Stress

Pronunciation

ca	=	ka	*like camera*
ça	=	sa	*like salary (façade)*
ce	=	se	*like celery*
ch	=	sh	*like champagne*
ci	=	si	*like citation*
co	=	ko	*like cola*
ço	=	so	*like solemn (garçon)*
cu	=	ku	*like cucumber*
çu	=	su	*like summer (aperçu)*
ga	=	ga	*like gas*
ge	=	zh	*like treasure*
gi	=	zh	*like mirage*
gn	=	nye	*like canyon or onion*
go	=	go	*like go*
gu	=	goo	*like goose*
h	=		*always silent in French*
j	=	zh	*like leisure (déjà vu, jeudi)*
[*j is always soft in French*]			
ll	=	lli	*like million*

ph	=	f	*like **phone***
s	=	s	*like possum*
sc	=	ss	*like **sc**ience*

[*sc* is **soft** when followed by *e* or *i*]

sc	=	sk	*like **sc**old*

[*sc* is **hard** when followed by *a, o* or *u*]

[*same rules as applied to *c* + **cedilla**, but **no cedilla** is required if *c* is **preceded** by *s*]

th	=	t	*like **t**ea*
tion	=	see-on	*like pronuncia**tion** (in French— no comparable sound in English)*
x	=	ks	*like ta**x***
	=	gs	*like e**x**ample*
y	=	ye	*like **y**et*
z	=	ze	*like **z**one*

Rules of Stress

■ Unlike English, which stresses the pronunciation of a specific syllable within a word, French syllables are evenly stressed. The last syllable of a word, however, is slightly emphasized.

NOTES

French syllables are evenly stressed, but the last syllable of the word is slightly emphasized.
(Unlike English, which stresses the pronunciation of a specific syllable within each word.)

Accent Marks

■ Accent marks consist of: **accent aigu, accent grave, accent circonflexe**, the **cédille** and the **tréma.**

◆ The **accent aigu** is used to open up the sound of a closed *e* when it is not followed by a final *d, f* or *z*: **café, répétez, vérité.**

◆ The **accent grave** is used:

• On an open *e* at the end of a syllable or before a final *s*: **mère, très.**

• To differentiate two homonyms (words spelled alike but which have a different meaning): **où** (*where*) and **ou** (*or*), à (**to, in, at**) and **a** (*has*), **là** (*there*) and **la** (*the*).

• On the vowel *a* in words such as **deçà, déjà, delà, voilà** (not in **cela**).

◆ The **accent circonflexe** is used on any of the five vowels:

• To indicate that a formerly used *vowel* or an *s* has been dropped: **bâtir** (*bastir*), **tête** (*teste*), **âge** (*eage*).

• To elongate the sound of certain vowels: **extrême, cône.**

• To differentiate two homonyms: **dû** (past participle of verb **devoir**) and **du** (contraction of **de** + **le**); **crû** (past participle of verb **croître**) and **cru** (past participle of verb **croire**); **mûr** (*ripe*) and **mur** (*wall*).

◆ The **tréma** is placed above the vowels *e, i, u* to indicate that they are pronounced independently of any preceding or following vowel sound: **Haïti, Noël.**

◆ The **cédille** is used beneath the letter *c* when it precedes the vowels *a, o, u* to give it an *s* sound: **façade, leçon, français.**

Examples:

Review of accent marks:

- **accent aigu** (acute accent) = é
- **accent grave** (grave accent) = à, è, ù
- **accent circonflexe** (circumflex) = â, ê, î, ô, û
- **accent tréma** (dieresis or umlaut) = ë, ï, ü
- **cédille** (cedilla) = ç

3 Numerals

Cardinals

0	zéro
1	un, une
2	deux
3	trois
4	quatre
5	cinq
6	six
7	sept
8	huit
9	neuf
10	dix
11	onze
12	douze
13	treize
14	quatorze
15	quinze
16	seize
17	dix-sept
18	dix-huit
19	dix-neuf
20	vingt

21	vingt et un
22	vingt-deux
23	vingt-trois
30	trente
31	trente et un
32	trente-deux
40	quarante
41	quarante et un
42	quarante-deux
50	cinquante
51	cinquante et un
52	cinquante-deux
60	soixante
61	soixante et un
62	soixante-deux
70	soixante-dix
71	soixante et onze
72	soixante-douze
80	quatre vingts
81	quatre-vingt-un
82	quatre-vingt-deux
90	quatre vingt-dix
91	quatre-vingt-onze
92	quatre-vingt-douze
100	cent
101	cent un
102	cent deux
200	deux cents
201	deux cent un
300	trois cents
1.000	mille

■ **Cent** and **mille** are expressed without an article.

■ The **-s** of **cents** is omitted if any other number follows: **cinq cents** *but* **cinq cent vingt.**

■ In France and in most other countries where the metric system of measurements is used, a comma is used to indicate a decimal while a period is used to indicate thousands, millions, etc.: **53.470,50** (instead of 53,470.50)

Ordinals

1st	**premier/première**
2nd	**deuxième**
3rd	**troisième**
4th	**quatrième**
5th	**cinquième**
6th	**sixième**
7th	**septième**
8th	**huitième**
9th	**neuvième**
10th	**dixième**
11th	**onzième**
12th	**douzième**
13th	**treizième**
14th	**quatorzième**
20th	**vingtième**
21st	**vingt et unième**

■ When expressing a date or the name of a monarch, only **premier/première** is used. Otherwise, a cardinal number is used: **le premier octobre** *but* **le onze mai; François Premier** *but* **Charles Cinq.**

■ An ordinal number is written by placing an elevated **e** next to the number: 3e (*3rd*), 15e (*15th*).

4 Nouns

Gender

■ French nouns are either feminine or masculine; in other words, they observe a gender difference. Of course, nouns that refer to males are usually masculine, and those that refer to females are usually feminine:

le garçon	the boy
la jeune fille	the girl
le livre	the book
la chaise	the chair

■ While there is no rule that determines why certain things are feminine and some masculine, some endings give a good indication of the gender of a word. The most common **masculine** noun endings are:

-age	le paysage
-aire	l'anniversaire

11

-at	le consulat
-èle	le parallèle
-eur	l'agriculteur
-exe	le complexe
-isme	le tourisme
-ment	le changement
-oir	le rasoir
-phone	le microphone
-scope	le magnétoscope

■ Days of the week, months, numbers, and the letters of the alphabet are masculine.

■ Names of most trees and bushes are masculine: **un rosier, un poirier.**

■ Soft drink trade names are masculine: **un Coca, un Perrier, un Orangina.**

■ Words borrowed from other languages are generally masculine: **le tennis, le parking.**

■ The most common feminine noun endings are:

-ade	la limonade
-aine	la laine
-ance	la naissance
-ence	la différence
-ère	la matière
-esse	la noblesse
-ette	la serviette
-euse	la danseuse

-ie	la boulangerie
-ise	la bêtise
-sion	la conversion
-ssion	la mission
-tion	la nation
-té	la fraternité
-trice	l'actrice
-ude	la solitude
-ure	la parure

■ Automobile trade names are feminine: **une Ford, une Peugeot.**

■ Names of most nuts and fruits are feminine: **une pistache, une poire.**

Plural
Common Nouns

■ An **-s** is added to most singular nouns to form their plural: **un livre/ des livres; une chaise/des chaises.**

■ If the noun already ends in **-s, -z or -x**, the plural form remains the same: **un fils/des fils; le nez/les nez; la croix/les croix.**

■ Most nouns ending in **-al** change to **-aux** : **un canal/des canaux; un cheval/des chevaux.**

　◆ Exceptions to this rule are several words which only add an **-s** to form their plural: **bal, cal, carnaval, chacal, festival, régal.**

■ Most nouns ending in **-au** or **-eu** form their plural by adding an **-x: un cheveu/des cheveux; un bureau/des bureaux.**

　◆ Exception: **un pneu/des pneus.**

■ Most nouns ending in **-ail** normally add an **-s** to form their plural. **un sérail/des sérails.**

◆ Exceptions to this rule are nine nouns which change **-ail** to **-aux** to form their plural: **bail/baux, corail/coraux, émail/émaux, soupirail/soupiraux, travail/travaux, vantail/vantaux, and vitrail/vitraux.**

■ Most nouns ending in **-ou** add an **-s** to form their plural: **un trou/des trous.**

◆ Exceptions are the following seven words which add an **-x:** **bijou/bijoux, caillou/cailloux, chou/choux, genou/genoux, hibou/hiboux, joujou/joujoux, and pou/poux.**

■ Some nouns have two forms for their plural forms, each form having a different meaning or usage: **aïeul/aïeuls/aïeux.**

Proper Nouns

■ They are expressed in the plural if they are:

◆ Nouns of nationality or world-renouned names: **les Bonapartes, les Russes.**

◆ Geographical names pertaining to several countries, mountains, etc.: **les Pyrenées, les Amériques.**

■ As a rule last names are not pluralized when they refer to:

◆ The entire family: **les Dupont, les Fortier.**

◆ Two or more individuals having the same name: **les deux Blanchard.**

Articles

5

NOTES

Articles agree in gender and number with the noun they modify.

Definite Articles

le	(masc. sing.)
la	(fem. sing.)
l'	(f./m. sing. before a vowel sound)
les	(f./m. plural)

■ All forms of the definite article mean *the*.

Indefinite Articles

un	(masc. sing.)
une	(fem. sing.)
des	(f./m. plural)

■ The English indefinite articles *a, an* do not have a true plural form. French does have the plural **des**, which has the meaning of *some*.

Partitive Articles

du	(masc. sing.)
de la	(fem. sing.)
de l'	(f./m. sing. before a vowel sound)
des	(f./m. plural)

■ Partitive articles are used to indicate a part or portion of a given quantity which is measurable but cannot be counted. They can be translated as *some* or *any*.

■ Indefinite and partitive articles **un, une, des, du, de la, de l'** change to **de** when they modify the direct object of a negative sentence: **Je mange** *des* **pommes / Je ne mange pas** *de* **pommes.**

Pronouns

6

Personal Pronouns

Singular		Plural	
je (j')	*(I)*	**nous**	*(we)*
tu	*(you, fam.)*	**vous**	*(you)*
il	*(he, it)*	**ils**	*(they - masc.)*
elle	*(she, it)*	**elles**	*(they - fem.)*
on	*(one, you, we, they)*		

■ The plural form **vous** is also used as a singular form to address an older person, someone in authority, or a stranger.

■ **Tu** is used for close friends, classmates and family.

■ **On** is an impersonal subject pronoun, and it is used very frequently in informal conversation: **On travaille beaucoup ici** *(One works a lot here)*. **On parle anglais aux États-Unis** *(They speak English in the United States)*. **Qu'est-ce qu'on fait ce soir?** *(What are we doing this evening?)*.

17

Disjunctive Pronouns

Singular		Plural	
moi	*(I, me)*	**nous**	*(us)*
toi	*(you)*	**vous**	*(you)*
lui	*(him)*	**eux**	*(them - masc.)*
elle	*(her)*	**elles**	*(them, - fem.)*

■ Disjunctive (stressed) pronouns are used:

◆ After a preposition: **pour moi** *(for me)*, **avec lui** *(with him)*, **après elle** *(after her)*.

◆ To emphasize a subject: **Moi, j'habite à Miami** *(I live in Miami)*.

◆ After **C'est** or **Ce sont**: **C'est moi qui parle français** *(It is I who speak French)*.

◆ As part of a compound subject: **Michèle et lui sortent demain** *(Michèle and he are going out tomorrow)*.

◆ In comparisons after **que: Ma soeur est plus jeune que moi** *(My sister is younger than I)*.

Direct Object Pronouns

Singular		Plural	
me (m')	*(me)*	**nous**	*(us)*
te (t')	*(you, sing. fam.)*	**vous**	*(you, pl. or sing. form.)*
le (l')	*(him, it)*	**les**	*(them)*
la (l')	*(her, it)*		

Indirect Object Pronouns

Singular		Plural	
me (m')	*(to me)*	**nous**	*(to us)*
toi	*(to you, sing. fam.)*	**vous**	*(to you, pl. or sing. form.)*
lui	*(to him, to her)*	**leur**	*(to them)*

Placement of Object Pronouns

■ A direct or an indirect object pronoun is placed:
   ◆ Before a conjugated verb: **Je mange la pomme** *(I eat the apple)*. **Je la mange** *(I eat it)*.
   ◆ Before the infinitive, when it is its object: **Il va étudier la leçon** *(He's going to study the lesson)*. **Il va l'étudier** *(He is going to study it)*.
   ◆ After an affirmative command, linked to it by a hyphen: **Parlez-lui!** *(Speak to him!)*.
     • **Me** and **te** become **moi** and **toi** when they follow an affirmative command.
   ◆ Before a negative command: **Ne la donne pas à Paul!** *(Don't give it to Paul)*.
■ When more than one object pronoun precedes the verb, the order of placement is:

me (m')	la (l')	lui		
te (t')	le (l')	leur	y	en
nous	les			
vous				

■ When they follow the verb, the order of placement is:

te (t')	moi (m')	nous		
la (l')	ltoi (t')	vous	y	en
les	lui	leur		

Adverbial Pronouns *Y & En*

■ The pronoun **y** is used to replace:

◆ A prepositional phrase, having the meaning of *at* or *to* a place; it is equivalent to the adverb **là: Je vais à la biblothèque** *(I'm going to the library).* **J'y vais** *(I'm going there).* **Elles habitent à Avignon** *(They live in Avignon).* **Elles y habitent** *(They live there).*

◆ A phrase consisting of **à** plus a noun, usually after verbs such as **réussir à, penser à, répondre à, jouer à: Il répond à ma lettre** *(He answers my letter).* **Il y répond** *(He answers it).*

• It is not used to replace a person, in which case an indirect object pronoun is used: **Elle répond au professeur** *(She answers the teacher).* **Elle lui répond** *(She answers him).*

■ The pronoun **en** is used to replace:

◆ A noun after the preposition **de: Nous arrivons de Madrid** *(We are arriving from Madrid).* **Nous en arrivons** *(We are arriving from there).*

◆ A phrase consisting of **de** plus a noun, usually after verbs such as **avoir besoin de, parler de, avoir envie de: Il a envie d'une limonade** *(He feels like [having] a lemonade).* **Il en a envie** *(He feels like [having] it).* **Isabelle a besoin d'argent** *(Isabelle needs money)* **Isabelle en a besoin** *(Isabelle needs it).*

◆ A phrase consisting of an indefinite or a partitive article: **Hervé a du chocolat** *(Hervé has some chocolate).* **Hervé en a** *(Hervé has some of it).*

◆ A phrase with a quantity expression or a number: **J'ai quatre livres de philosophie** *(I have four philosophy books).* **J'en ai quatre** *(I have four of them).* **Combien de bouteilles est-ce que vous voulez?** *(How many bottles do you want?)* **J'en veux cinq** *(I want five of them).*

■ **Y** and **en** are placed in a sentence following the placement rules for the direct and indirect object pronouns.

■ When **y** or **en** follow an affirmative command of an **-er** ending verb in the **tu** person, the final **-s** is not omitted, as is the case otherwise: **Va au laboratoire!** *(Go to the lab!)* **Vas-y!** *(Go there!)* **Parle de ton voyage!** *(Talk about your trip!)* **Parles-en!** *(Talk about it!)*

Reflexive Pronouns

me (m')	nous
te (t')	vous
se (s')	se (s')

■ Reflexive pronouns are used with pronominal verbs in addition to the subject pronoun and agree with the subject of the verb: **Je me lave** *(I wash [myself]).* **Il se réveille** *(He wakes [himself] up).*

■ **Me, te, se** become **m', t', s'** before a vowel or non-aspirate **h: Tu t'arrêtes toujours devant la pâtisserie** *(You always stop in front of the pastry shop).*

■ **Te** becomes **toi** when used in the affirmative imperative: **Dépêche-toi!** *(Hurry up!)*.

■ Their position in relation to the verb is the same as indirect and direct object pronouns: **Je me demande** *(I wonder)*. **Je me suis rappelé** *(I remembered)*. **Je vais m'excuser** *(I am going to excuse myself)*.

Demonstrative Pronouns

Masculine		Feminine	Neuter	
celui	*(singular)*	**celle**	**ce**	*(this one, that one, the one)*
ceux	*(plural)*	**celles**	**ce**	*(these, those, the ones)*

■ Demonstrative pronouns are used in one of three instances:
  ◆ With the suffix **-ci or -là: Je préfère celle-ci et ceux-là** *(I prefer this one [fem.] and those [masc.])*.
  ◆ Followed by a clause beginning with a relative pronoun: **Ceux qui étudient beaucoup vont avoir de bonnes notes** *(Those who study hard are going to have good grades)*. **Ce que je vais te dire n'est pas très agréable** *(That which I am going to tell you is not very nice)*.
  ◆ Followed by a prepositional phrase that usually begins with **de: Celles de mes étudiantes qui vont en France ont fait leurs devoirs tout de suite.** *(Those of my students who are going to France did their homework right away)*.

There are three *indefinite* demonstrative pronouns: **ceci, cela** and **ça**: **Ceci est très important** *(This is very important).* **Tu aimes cela?** *(Do you like that?)* **Ça, c'est formidable!** *(That's great!)*

Possessive Pronouns

Singular

Masculine	Feminine	
le mien	la mienne	*(mine)*
le tien	la tienne	*(yours, sing. fam.)*
le sien	la sienne	*(his, hers)*
le nôtre	la nôtre	*(ours)*
le vôtre	la vôtre	*(yours, pl. or sing. form.)*
le leur	la leur	*(theirs)*

Examples:
- **C'est ma mère ici** *(It's my mother here).*
- **Où est la tienne?** *(Where is yours?)*
- **Mes étudiants sont vieux que les vôtres.** *(My students are older than yours).*

Plural

Masculine	Feminine	
les miens	les miennes	*(mine)*
les tiens	les tiennes	*(yours, sing. fam.)*
les siens	les siennes	*(his, hers)*
les nôtres	(same)	*(ours)*
les vôtres	(same)	*(yours, pl. or sing. form.)*
les leurs	(same)	*(theirs)*

Adjectives

NOTES

Adjectives modify (describe) nouns and pronouns.

Descriptive Adjectives

■ Must agree in gender and number with the noun or pronoun modified.

■ Most masculine adjectives may be changed to the feminine by adding an **-e: intelligent/ intelligente; américain/américaine; grand/grande.**

■ Some adjectives have the same form for both masculine and feminine: **calme, optimiste, pessimiste, avare, riche, excentrique, sociable,** etc.

■ Irregular adjective feminine endings include: **-el** to **-elle (mutuel/mutuelle); -eur, -eux** to **-euse (paresseux/paresseuse); -er** to **-ère (cher/chère); -ien** to **-ienne (canadien/ canadienne); -if** to **-ive (destructif/destructive); -il** to **ille (pareil/pareille).**

■ Most adjectives of color have a masculine and a feminine form: **blanc/blanche, bleu/bleue, gris/grise, vert/verte, violet/violette;** those that end in a mute *e* have a single form shared by both masculine and feminine nouns: **jaune, rose, rouge.**

◆ Two adjectives of color do not change, regardless of gender or number: **marron** and **orange.**

■ Most descriptive adjectives, including those of nationality and color, are placed after the noun. Exceptions are **autre, beau/belle, bon(ne), chaque, faux/fausse, gentil(le), grand(e), gros(se), jeune, joli(e), long(ue), nouveau/nouvelle, mauvais(e), pauvre, petit(e), vieux/vieille, vrai(e): un garçon intelligent/un jeune garçon.**

■ Before a word beginning with a vowel sound, **beau** changes to **bel, nouveau** to **nouvel, vieux** to **vieil: un nouveau restaurant / un bel hôtel.**

■ The descriptive adjectives **ancien(ne), grand(e), pauvre,** and **cher/chère** may be used either before or after the noun they modify, but their meaning changes according to their position: **une maison ancienne** *(an old house)*/**un ancien professeur** *(a former professor)*; **une grande actrice** *(a great actress)*/**une actrice grande** *(a tall actress)*; **le pauvre homme** *(the poor [unfortunate] man)*/ **l'homme pauvre** *(the poor [without money] man)*; **ma chère mère** *(my dear mother)*/**une voiture chère** *(an expensive car)*.

■ If a plural noun used in the partitive is preceded by an adjective, the partitive article **des** changes to **de: Nous avons des livres français** *(We have French books).* **J'ai acheté de belles pommes** *(I bought beautiful apples).*

■ When a noun is modified by more than one adjective, the above rules are observed for each particular adjective: **C'est une petite maison blanche et bleue** *(It's a little white and blue house).*

Demonstrative Adjectives

Point out a person, object, idea, or point in time.

ce	masc. sing. before a consonant: **ce restaurant** (*this restaurant*)
cet	masc. sing. before a vowel or mute h: **cet étudiant** (*this student*)
cette	fem sing.: **cette étudiante** (*this student*), **cette chaise** (*this chair*)
ces	masc./fem. plural: **ces hôtels** (*these hotels*), **ces livres** (*these books*), **ces robes** (*these dresses*)

■ To indicate the relative distance between the speaker and what is spoken of, the suffixes **-ci** (for something close) and **-là** (for something further away) are added to the noun: **cette bouteille-ci** *(this bottle)*; **ces crayons-ci** *(these pencils)*; **cette chaise-là** *(that chair)*, **ces magasins-là** *(those stores)*.

Possessive Adjectives

Masculine Singular	Feminine Singular	M/F Plural
mon	**ma**	**mes** (*my*)
ton	**ta**	**tes** (*your*)
son	**sa**	**ses** (*his, her*)
notre	**notre**	**nos** (*our*)
votre	**votre**	**vos** (*your*)
leur	**leur**	**leurs** (*their*)

- Agree in gender and number with the noun modified –not with the possessor, but with what is possessed: **sa mère** *(his/her mother)*; **mon livre** *(my book)*; **ses étudiantes** *(his/her students [f.])*; **nos ordinateurs** *(our computers)*; **son fils** *(his/her son)*.
- **Ma, ta, sa** change to the masculine forms **mon, ton, son** when the following word begins with a vowel sound: **mon amie, ton étudiante, son église**

Interrogative Adjectives

Used to ask questions or get more precise information about a noun

quel	masc. sing.
quelle	fem. sing.
quels	masc. plural
quelles	fem. plural

- They are followed by the noun they modify or by the verb être and the noun it modifies: **Quelle est la nationalité de ton professeur?** *(What is your teacher's nationality?)*
- They are translated as *which*? but also as *what*? in certain expressions such as: **Quelle heure est-il?** *(What time is it?)* **Quelle est la date aujourd'hui?** *(What is the date today?)* **Quelle est l'adresse de notre professeur?** *(What is our teacher's address?)* **Quel jour sommes-nous?** *(What day is it?)*

Common Adjectives

Add (-s) for plurals—irregular plurals are listed

	masculin/féminin
affectionate	**affectueux/-se**
ambitious	**ambitieux/-euse**

	masculin/féminin
anxious	**anxieux/-euse**
athletic	**sportif/-ive**
beautiful	**beau/belle**
blond	**blond/e**
brunette	**brun/ne**
calm	**calme**
comfortable	**confortable**
cute	**mignon/ne**
difficult	**difficile**
divorced	**divorcé/e**
elegant	**élégant/e**
embarrassed	**embarrassé/-e**
energetic	**énergique**
faithful	**fidèle**
fantastic	**formidable**
fat	**gros/se**
funny	**amusant/e**
furious	**furieux/se**
generous	**généreux/-se**
gentle	**doux/douce**
gifted	**doué/e**
good	**bon/ne**
happy	**heureux/-se**
jealous	**jaloux/-se**
lazy	**paresseux/-euse**
likeable	**sympathique**
married	**marié/e**
mean	**méchant/e**
medium	**moyen/ne**

	masculin/féminin
nice/kind	**gentil/le**
new	**nouveau/-elle**
old	**vieux/vieille**
pleasant	**agréable**
polite	**poli/e**
practical	**pratique**
pretty	**joli/e**
reasonable	**raisonnable**
remarried	**remarié/e**
reserved	**réservé/e**
sad	**triste**
sensitive	**sensible**
serious	**sérieux/-se**
short	**court/e**
shy	**timide**
stern	**sévère**
strange	**étrange**
stressed	**stressé/e**
strong	**fort/e**
stubborn	**têtu/e**
stupid	**stupide**
surprised	**surpris/e**
tall	**grand/e**
tender	**tendre**
thin (slender)	**mince**
tiresome	**pénible**
unhappy	**malheureux/-se**
well	**en forme**
worried	**inquiet/e**
young	**jeune**

8
Comparatives & Superlatives

Comparatives

■ Adjectives and adverbs form their comparative of superiority, of inferiority and of equality in the same fashion:

$$\left.\begin{array}{l} \textbf{plus} \\ \textbf{moins} \\ \textbf{aussi} \end{array}\right\} \text{(adjective/adverb)} \quad \textbf{que}$$

Marie est plus belle que Jeanne (*Marie is more beautiful than Jeanne*). **Robert parle moins vite que Charles** (*Robert speaks less fast than Charles*). **Hélène est aussi intelligente que son frère** (*Helen is as intelligent as her brother*).

◆ The compared adjective agrees in gender and number with the subject of the sentence.

■ Nouns are compared as follows:

$$\left.\begin{array}{l} \textbf{plus de} \\ \textbf{moins de} \\ \textbf{autant de} \end{array}\right\} \text{(noun)} \quad \textbf{que}$$

J'ai plus de patience que ma cousine (*I have more patience than my cousin*). **Tu as moins**

d'argent que ta mère (*You have less money than your mother*). **Patrice a autant de cours que moi** (*Patrice has as many courses as I*).

◆ When numbers are compared, **de** is used instead of **que**: **Il a plus de quatre amis** (*He has more than four friends*). **Céline a moins de trente euros** (*Céline has less than thirty euros*).

■ The adjective **bon/bonne** and adverb **bien** have irregular comparative and superlative forms. Note that in English they share the same comparative and superlative forms, but not in French:

bon(s), bonne(s)	*good*
meilleur(s), meilleure(s)	*better*
le(s) meilleur(s), meilleure(s)	*the best*
bien	*well*
mieux	*better*
le mieux	*best*

◆ The regular forms **plus mauvais(e), plus mal**, etc. are also acceptable.

■ The adjective **mauvais/mauvaise** and the adverb **mal** also have optional comparative and superlative forms:

mauvais(e/es)	*bad*
pire	*worse*
le, la/les pire(s)	*the worst*
mal	*badly*
pis	*worse*
le pis	*worst*

■ The indefinite articles **un/une** are used in the comparative; the definite articles **le/la/les** are used in the superlative: **une meilleure voiture** (*a better automobile*); **la meilleure voiture** (*the best automobile*).

Superlatives

■ The superlative of superiority or inferiority of adjectives is formed by adding the corresponding definite article in front of the comparative form of the adjective if it precedes the noun: **le plus bel enfant** (*the most beautiful child*), **la plus grande maison** (*the biggest house*).

■ If the adjective follows the noun, a second definite article is used in front of the noun: **la jeune fille la plus intelligente/le garçon le plus intelligent** (*the most intelligent girl/boy*); **la leçon la moins intéressante/le roman le moins intéressant** (*the least interesting lesson/novel*).

■ The superlative of superiority or inferiority of adverbs is formed by adding the invariable article **le** in front of the comparative form: **Francine parle le plus vite** (*Francine speaks the fastest*). **Robert travaille le moins vite** (*Robert works the least fast*).

■ The preposition **de** is used when a specific category is mentioned. It translates as *in*: **C'est la jeune fille la plus intelligente de la classe** (*She is the most intelligent girl in the class*). **Michèle lit le plus vite de la classe** (*Michèle reads the fastest in the class*).

Adverbs

NOTES

Adverbs modify (describe) verbs, adjectives or other adverbs.

Examples:
- *Adverb* modifying a <u>verb</u>: **Elle <u>*chante*</u> bien.** (She <u>*sings*</u> well.)
- *Adverb* modifying an <u>adjective</u>: **C'est un livre *très <u>intéressant</u>*.** (That's a *very <u>interesting</u>* book.)
- *Adverb* modifying <u>another adverb</u>: **L'instituteur parle *très* <u>vite</u>.** (The teacher speaks *very* <u>quickly</u>.)

■ **Elle chante bien** (*She sings well*). **C'est un livre très intéressant** (*That's a very interesting book*). **L'instituteur parle très vite** (*The teacher speaks very fast*).
◆ Most adverbs immediately follow conjugated (or inflected) verbs but precede adjectives and adverbs: **Tu parles bien** (*You speak well*). **Tu as bien parlé** (*You spoke well*).
◆ Adverbial phrases and adverbs of time are usually placed at the beginning or at the end of the

sentence: **Aujourd'hui nous allons au musée** (*Today we are going to the museum*). **Elles vont en Europe de temps en temps** (*They go to Europe from time to time*).

■ While many adverbs do not derive from adjectives, many of them are formed by adding the suffix **-ment** to certain adjectives:

◆ An adjective ending in **-e** just adds **-ment: rarement, probablement.**

◆ An adjective ending in a consonant in the masculine is changed to its feminine form before adding **-ment: fortement, certainement, silencieusement.**

◆ Sometimes an accent aigu is placed on the **-e** before adding the suffix: **énormément, precisément.**

◆ An adjective ending in **-ant** substitutes **-amment** to form an adverb: **élégant/élégamment; courant/couramment.**

◆ An adjective ending in **-ent** substitutes **-emment** to form an adverb: **récent/récemment; évident/ évidemment.**

Examples:
Many adverbs do not derive from adjectives, for example: **bien** *(well)*; **beaucoup** *(a lot)*; **peu** *(little)*; **mal** *(bad)*; **déjà** *(already)*; **assez** *(enough)*; **vite** *(quickly)*; **plutôt** *(rather)*; **très** *(very)*.

Common Adverbs

a lot, much	**beaucoup**
almost	**presque**
already	**déjà**
also	**aussi**
always	**toujours**
as much	**autant**
badly	**mal**
best	**le mieux**
better	**mieux**
enough	**assez**
late	**tard**
little	**peu**
often	**souvent**
quickly	**vite**
rather	**plutôt**
so much	**tant**
sometimes	**quelquefois**
soon	**bientôt**
still	**encore**
together	**ensemble**
too much	**trop**
very	**très**
well	**bien**
worse	**pire**
worst	**le pire**

Prepositions

NOTES
Prepositions connect nouns and pronouns to other words.

Prepositions to Remember

à*	to, toward
après	after
avec	with
chez	at, at the home of
contre	against; in exchange for
dans	in, into; within
de*	of, from; about
depuis	from, since
derrière	behind
dès	from, since
dévant	before, in front of
durant	for, during, while

* **à** and **de** take these contracted forms with the articles **le** and **les**: *au, aux du, des*

en	in, inside (also an adverbial pronoun)
entre	between
jusque	until
par	per, through, by
pour	for, in order to
près	nearby
sans	without
sauf	without, except for
selon	according to
sous	below, under, beneath
sur	over, above; about
suivant	according to
vers	to, toward

Examples:
- **Ils voyagent en Angleterre.** (*They are traveling in England.*)
- **Mon frère va passer une année en Chine.** (*My brother is going to spend a year in China.*)
- **Il est parti aux États-Unis.** (*He left for the United States.*)

Some verbs require a preposition (usually **à** or **de**) before an infinitive; others do not. (It is best to learn the verb along with the preposition.)

Some Verbs That Take À

aider à	to help
apprendre à	to learn
arriver à	to arrive
commencer à	to begin
continuer à	to continue
hésiter à	to hesitate
inviter à	to invite
parvenir à	to reach
réussir à	to succeed

Some Verbs That Take DE

continuer de	to continue
décider de	to decide
se dépêcher de	to hurry up
essayer de	to attempt, try
finir de	to end, finish
oublier de	to forget
refuser de	to refuse
regretter de	to regret

Verbs
The Basics

11

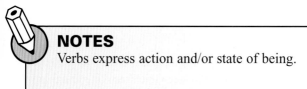

NOTES
Verbs express action and/or state of being.

Verb Overview

■ Infinitive
- ◆ Form of a verb which shows *no subject* or *number*. It is usually preceded in English by the preposition "to."
- ◆ In French, infinitives have four possible endings: **-er, -ir, -oir**, and **-re**: **parler** (*to speak*), **finir** (*to finish*), **voir** (*to see*), **prendre** (*to take*).

■ Past Participle
- ◆ Form of a verb used either as an *adjective* or together *with an auxiliary verb* (**ÊTRE** or **AVOIR**) to form the compound tenses. [Their formation is shown on p. 45, under **past participle**.]

■ Present Participle
- ◆ Form of a verb corresponding to the English form ending in **-ing**.
- ◆ Present participles are formed in French by taking the nous form of the present indicative tense, dropping the **-ons** ending, and adding **-ant**: **parlant, finissant, perdant.**

◆ The two most commonly used irregular present participles are **avoir/ayant, savoir/sachant**.

Infinitive

■ *The most basic form of the verb, such as* **chanter** *(to sing),* **finir** *(to end),* **prendre** *(to take),* **voir** *(to see)*

◆ Verbs are composed of a stem or radical: The first portion of the verb, such as **chant-, fin-, prend-**

◆ And infinitive ending: the last letters in the verb, such as **-er, -ir, -re, -oir**. The stem or radical and the ending create the verb: **chanter, finir, prendre, voir,** etc...

◆ Verbs are usually conjugated by removing the infinitive ending and applying a new ending, corresponding to a certain set of rules.

◆ There are six different endings, one for each subject pronoun:

• To use the verb **chanter** in the simple tense, take the stem **chant-** and attach the ending according to the following rules.

  For present tense:

  > **Je:** (first-person, singular subject pronoun) **chant+e**—*I sing*

  > **Tu:** (second-person, singular familiar subject pronoun) **chant+es**—*you sing*

  > **Il:** (third-person, singular, male subject pronoun) **chant+e**—*he sings*

  > **Elle:** (third-person, singular female subject pronoun) **chant+e**—*she sings*

  > **Nous:** (first-person, plural, male and female subject pronoun) **chant+ons**—*we sing*

  > **Vous:** (second-person, plural, male and

female subject pronoun), and also (second-person, singular, male and female, formal subject pronoun) **chant+ez**—*you sing*
> **Ils:** (third-person, plural, male subject pronoun) **chant+ent**—*they sing*
> **Elles:** (third-person, plural, female subject pronoun) **chant+ent**—*they sing*

Past Participle
■ Used to form the perfect tenses, with the auxiliary (helping) verb **AVOIR** or **ÊTRE**
■ Also used to serve as an adjective, always agreeing in gender and number with the noun being modified **le travail fini** (*the finished work*)
■ Also used to form the passive voice:
◆ Regular -er verbs: **Chant+é, és, ée, ées**
◆ Regular -ir verbs: **Fin+i, is, ie, ies**

Present Participle
■ Equivalent to the English **-ing** form of verbs (*singing, ending*)
■ Formation: drop the ending **-ons** from the first person plural of the present tense and add **-ant**
■ Regular -er verbs: **chant+ant** (*singing*)
Elle lave la vaisselle en chantant.
(*She sings while doing the dishes.*)
■ Regular -ir verbs: **finiss+ant** (*finishing*)
Il chante en finissant ses devoirs.
(*He sings while finishing his homework.*)
■ Some irregular present participles: **avoir: ayant** (*having*); **être: étant** (*being*); **savoir: sachant** (*knowing*); **voir: voyant**(*seeing*); **aller: allant** (*going*).

Moods
■ **Indicative**
  ◆ Most commonly used mood.
  ◆ Expresses facts and actual situations. (Unless another mood is specified, the mood used for tense conjugations is the indicative.)
■ **Subjunctive**
  ◆ Used to express actions that are doubtful, possible or wished for.
  ◆ Follows expressions of feelings, opinions, attitudes or doubts.
  ◆ Always introduced by **QUE.**
■ **Imperative**
  ◆ Used to express orders (commands).

Conjugations

Examples:
Verbs are conjugated to match pronouns:
- **je (j'** before vowel)   (I)
- **tu**   (you, fam. sing.)
- **vous**   (you, form. sing.)
- **il, elle**   (he, she, it)
- **nous**   (we)
- **vous**   (you, fam. pl.)
- **ils, elles**   (they)

■ According to infinitive endings: **-er, -ir, -re**
  ◆ Most verb forms are created by dropping the infinitive ending (leaving the infinitive stem) and adding other endings.
  ◆ Verbs following these general formation rules are called **regular verbs.**
■ Different endings
  ◆ Depend on mood, tense or person of verb.

12 **Regular Verbs**

NOTES

To review, as mentioned in chapter 11, most verb forms are created by dropping the infinitive ending (leaving the infinitive stem) and adding other endings. Verbs that following these basic formation rules are called regular verbs.

-er verbs

Verbs ending in **-er** are the most common, they follow the same conjugation as the verb **chanter.**

Common **-er** verbs

■ **chercher:**   to look for
■ **danser:**   to dance
■ **demander:**   to ask
■ **donner:**   to give
■ **fermer:**   to close
■ **jouer:**   to play
■ **laver:**   to wash
■ **louer:**   to rent
■ **marcher:**   to walk
■ **montrer:**   to show
■ **parler:**   to speak
■ **refuser:**   to refuse
■ **regarder:**   to look at

- ■ **rencontrer:**   to meet
- ■ **rester:**   to stay
- ■ **sauter:**   to jump
- ■ **tomber:**   to fall
- ■ **toucher:**   to touch
- ■ **travailler:**   to work

-ir verbs

With an infinitive ending in **-ir**, and also a present participle ending in **-issant**, they follow the same conjugation as the verbe **finir.**

Common -ir verbs

- ■ **accomplir:**   to accomplish
- ■ **choisir:**   to choose
- ■ **envahir:**   to invade
- ■ **finir:**   to finish
- ■ **remplir:**   to fill

-re verbs

With an infinitive ending in **-re:**

Common -re verbs

- ■ **attendre:**   to wait for
- ■ **entendre:**   to hear
- ■ **perdre:**   to lose
- ■ **rendre:**   to give back
- ■ **vendre:**   to sell

Simple Tenses

Present

- ■ Regular **-er** verbs

  chanter (to sing):

chant+**e**	chant+**ons**
chant+**es**	chant+**ez**
chant+**e**	chant+**ent**

  Elle chante bien. (*She sings well.*)

■ Regular **-ir** verbs

fin+**is**	fin+**issons**
fin+**is**	fin+**issez**
fin+**it**	fin+**issent**

Ils finissent le livre. *(They finish the book.)*

Imperfect

■ Regular **-er** verbs

chant+**ais**	chant+**ions**
chant+**ais**	chant+**iez**
chant+**ait**	chant+**aient**

Elle chantait bien. *(She sang well.)*

■ Regular **-ir** verbs

fin+**issais**	fin+**issions**
fin+**issais**	fin+**issiez**
fin+**issait**	fin+**issaient**

Ils finissaient le livre. *(They finished the book)*

Simple Past

■ Regular **-er** verbs

chant+**ai**	chant+**âmes**
chant+**as**	chant+**âtes**
chant+**a**	chant+**èrent**

Elle chanta bien. *(She sang well.)*

■ Regular **-ir** verbs

fin+**is**	fin+**îmes**
fin+**is**	fin+**îtes**
fin+**it**	fin+**irent**

Ils finirent le livre. *(They finished the book.)*

Future

■ Regular **-er** verbs

chanter+**ai**	chanter+**ons**
chanter+**as**	chanter+**ez**
chanter+**a**	chanter+**ont**

Elle chantera bien. *(She will sing well.)*

■ Regular **-ir** verbs

finir+**ai**	finir+**ons**
finir+**as**	finir+**ez**
finir+**a**	finir+**ont**

   Ils finiront le livre. *(They will finish the book.)*

Conditional

■ Regular **-er** verbs

chanter+**ais**	chanter+**ions**
chanter+**ais**	chanter+**iez**
chanter+**ait**	chanter+**aient**

   Elle chanterait bien. *(She would sing well.)*

■ Regular **-ir** verbs

finir+**ais**	finir+**ions**
finir+**ais**	finir+**iez**
finir+**ait**	finir+**aient**

   Ils finiraient le livre. *(They would finish the book.)*

Subjunctive Present

Follows expressions of attitudes, opinion, doubts feelings and is introduced by **QUE**. The subjunctive is used after:

■ Verbs of wishing, desire, or will:

aimer que...	*to love that...*
désirer que...	*to desire that...*
souhaiter que...	*to wish that...*

   Je souhaite que tu finisses le livre.
   (*I wish that you finish the book.*)

■ Expressions of emotion, opinion, doubt, such as:

être heureux que...	*to be happy that...*
être triste que...	*to be sad that...*
être surpris que...	*to be surprised that...*
avoir peur que...	*to be afraid that...*

   Nous sommes surpris qu'elle chante bien.
   (*We are surprised that she sings well.*)

■ Expressions of necessity and obligation, such as:

il faut que... *must...*
il est essentiel que... *it is essential that...*
il est nécessaire que... *it is necessary that...*

Il faut que nous finissions le livre.
(*We must finish the book.*)

■ Regular **-er** verbs

chant+**e**   chant+**ions**
chant+**es**   chant+**iez**
chant+**e**   chant+**ent**

Il faut qu'elle chante bien.
(*She must sing well.*)

■ Regular **-ir** verbs

fin+**isse**   fin+**issions**
fin+**isses**   fin+**issiez**
fin+**isse**   fin+**issent**

Je souhaite qu'ils finissent le livre.
(*I wish that they would finish the book.*)

Perfect Tenses

Perfect tenses are formed with conjugated helping verbs:
AVOIR (*to have*) or **ÊTRE** (*to be*) + past participle.

Formation of Perfect Tenses
Use the auxiliary (helping) verb
AVOIR or ÊTRE + past participle

■ **ÊTRE** used with:

◆ Pronominal (reflexive) forms
Les filles se sont regardées.
(*The girls looked at each other.*)

◆ Verbs of motion, such as: **aller**, *to go*; **venir**, *to come*; **revenir**, *to come back*; **devenir,** *to become*; **rester**, *to stay*; **retourner**, *to return*; **arriver**, *to arrive*; **partir**, *to leave*; **tomber**, *to* *fall*; **monter**, *to go up*; **descendre**, *to go down*; **devenir**, *to become*; **entrer**, *to enter*; **sortir**, *to go out*; **naitre**, *to be born*; **mourir**, *to die*, etc...

Elle est tombée dans l'escalier.

   (*She fell in the stairs.*)

◆ **ÊTRE** + past participle of the verb:

   Elle est   allée au restaurant.

   (*She went to the restaurant.*)

■ **AVOIR** is used with all other verbs.

   ◆ **AVOIR** + past participle of the verb:

   Elle a lavé la voiture.

   (*She washed the car* = no agreement with subject nor object)

   Elle l' a lavée.

   (agrees in gender and number with a direct object [**l' = la voiture**] if placed before the verb)

Present Perfect

■ Use the following conjugation of **AVOIR** + past participle: **j'ai, tu as, il/ elle a, nous avons, vous avez, ils/ elles ont.**

   Elle a regardé un film.

   (*She watched a movie.*)

■ Or use the following conjugation of **ÊTRE** + past participle: **je suis, tu es, il/elle est, nous sommes, vous êtes, ils /elles sont.**

   Elles sont allées au restaurant.

   (*They went to the restaurant.*)

Past Perfect

■ Use the following conjugation of **AVOIR** + past participle: **j'avais, tu avais, il/ elle avait, nous avions, vous aviez, ils /elles avaient.**

   Elle avait regardé un film.

   (*She had watched a movie.*)

■ Or use the following conjugation of **ÊTRE** + past participle: **j'étais, tu étais, il/elle était, nous étions, vous étiez, ils/elles étaient.**

Past Anterior

■ Use the following conjugation of **AVOIR** + past participle: **j'eus, tu eus, il/elle eut, nous eûmes, vous eûtes, ils/elles eurent.**

Elle eut regardé un film.

(*She had watched a movie.*)

■ Or use the following conjugation of **ÊTRE** + past participle: **je fus, tu fus, il/elle fut, nous fûmes, vous fûtes, ils/elles furent.**

Elles furent allées au restaurant.

(*They went to the restaurant.*)

Future Perfect

■ Use the following conjugation of **AVOIR** + past participle: **j'aurai, tu auras, il/elle aura, nous aurons, vous aurez, ils/elles auront.**

Elle aura regardé un film.

(*She will have watched a movie.*)

■ Or use the following conjugation of **ÊTRE** + past participle: **je serai, tu seras, il/elle sera, nous serons, vous serez, ils/elles seront.**

Elles seront allées au restaurant.

(*They will have gone to the restaurant.*)

Conditional Perfect

■ Use the following conjugation of **AVOIR** + past participle: **j'aurais, tu aurais, il/elle aurait, nous aurions, vous auriez, ils/elles auraient.**

■ Or use the following conjugation of **ÊTRE** + past participle: **je serais, tu serais, il/elle serait, nous serions, vous seriez, ils/elles seraient.**

Subjunctive Perfect

Follows expressions of attitudes, opinion, doubts feelings and is introduced by **QUE** in the same way as the present subjunctive.

- Use the following conjugation of **AVOIR** + past participle: **j'aie, tu aies, il/elle ait, nous ayons, vous ayez, ils/elles aient.**
- Or use the following conjugation of **ÊTRE**: **je sois, tu sois, il/elle soit, nous soyons, vous soyez, ils/ elles soient.**

Subjunctive Pluperfect

Follows expressions of attitudes, opinion, doubts feelings and is introduced by **QUE:**

- Use the following conjugation of **AVOIR**: **j'eusse, tu eusses, il/elle eût, nous eussions, vous eussiez, ils/elles eussent.**
- Or use the following conjugation of **ÊTRE**: **je fusse, tu fusses, il/elle fût, nous fussions, vous fussiez, ils/elles fussent.**

NOTES

Perfect and pluperfect subjunctive are literary tenses and are rarely used.

13

Irregular Verbs

-ir Verbs

■ **acceuillir**	to welcome
■ **ceuillir**	to pick, to gather
■ **couvrir**	to cover
■ **offrir**	to offer
■ **ouvrir**	to open
■ **souffrir**	to suffer

-oir Verbs

■ **croire**	to believe
■ **recevoir**	to receive
■ **revoir**	to see again
■ **voir**	to see

-re Verbs

■ **apprendre**	to learn
■ **comprendre**	to understand
■ **prendre**	to take
■ **reprendre**	to take back

> *Examples:*
> Some of the most useful verbs are irregular:
> **dire** (*to say*), **faire** (*to do, to make*), **aller** (*to go*), **venir** (*to come*), **entendre** (*to hear*), **pouvoir** (*to be able*), **mettre** (*to put*), **sortir** (*to exit*), **partir** (*to leave*), **voir** (*to see*), **savoir** (*to know*), **boire** (*to drink*), etc...

Simple Tenses

The following are used as examples: **tenir** (*to hold*) **lire** (*to read*) **voir** (to see) **aller** (*to go*)

Present

■ **tenir**

tiens	tenons
tiens	tenez
tient	tiennent

    Je tiens le parapluie. (*I hold the umbrella.*)

■ **lire**

lis	lisons
lis	lisez
lit	lisent

    Je lis le journal. (*I read the newspaper.*)

■ **voir**

vois	voyons
vois	voyez
voit	voient

    Je vois le film. (*I see the movie.*)

■ **aller**

vais	allons
vas	allez
va	vont

    Je vais au restaurant. (*I go to the restaurant.*)

Imperfect
■ **tenir**

tenais	tenions
tenais	teniez
tenait	tenaient

Je tiens le parapluie. (*I hold the umbrella.*)

■ **lire**

lisais	lisions
lisais	lisiez
lisait	lisaient

Je lisais le journal. (*I read the newspaper.*)

■ **voir**

voyais	voyions
voyais	voyiez
voyait	voyaient

Je voyais le film. (*I saw the movie.*)

■ **aller**

allais	allions
allais	alliez
allait	allaient

J' allais au restaurant. (*I went to the restaurant.*)

Simple Past
■ **tenir**

tins	tenâmes
tins	tenâtes
tint	tinrent

Je tins le parapluie. (*I held the umbrella.*)

■ **lire**

lis	lisâmes
lis	lisâtes
lit	lisèrent

Je lis le journal. (*I read the newspaper.*)

■ **voir**

vis	vîmes

vis	vîtes
vit	virent

Je vis le film. (*I saw the movie.*)

■ **aller**

allai	allâmes
allas	allâtes
alla	allèrent

Je allai au restaurant. (*I went to the restaurant.*)

Future

■ **tenir**

tiendrai	tiendrons
tiendras	tiendrez
tiendra	tiendront

Je tiendrai le parapluie.
(*I will hold the umbrella.*)

■ **lire**

lirai	lirons
liras	lirez
lira	liront

Je lirai le journal. (*I will read the newspaper.*)

■ **voir**

verrai	verrons
verras	verrez
verra	verront

Je verrai le film. (*I will see the movie.*)

■ **aller**

irai	irons
iras	irez
ira	iront

J'irai au restaurant. (*I will go to the restaurant.*)

Conditional

■ **tenir**

tiendrais	tiendrions
tiendrais	tiendriez
tiendrait	tiendraient

Je tiendrais le parapluie.
  (*I would hold the umbrella.*)

■ **lire**

lirais	lirions
lirais	liriez
lirait	liraient

  Je lirais le journal. (*I would read the newspaper.*)

■ **voir**

verrais	verrions
verrais	verriez
verrait	verraient

  Je verrais le film. (*I would see the movie.*)

■ **aller**

irais	irions
irais	riez
irait	iraient

  J'irais au restaurant. (*I would go to the restaurant.*)

Subjunctive Present

■ **tenir**

tienne	tenions
tiennes	teniez
tienne	tiennent

  Il faut que je tienne le parapluie.
  (*I must hold the umbrella.*)

■ **lire**

lise	lisions
lises	lisiez
lise	lisent

  Il faut que je lise le journal.
  (*I must read the newspaper.*)

■ **voir**

voie	voyions
voies	voyiez

voie   voient

Il faut que je voie le film. (*I must see the movie.*)

■ **aller**

aille   allions

ailles   alliez

aille   aillent

Il faut que j'aille au restaurant.

(I must go to the restaurant.)

Perfect Tenses

Formation of Perfect Tenses

■ Both regular and irregular verbs have the same rules for perfect tenses.

■ They use the auxiliary (helping) verb

AVOIR or ÊTRE + past participle

■ **ÊTRE** is used with:

◆ Pronominal (reflexive) forms

◆ Verbs of motion such as: **aller** (*to go*), **venir** (*to come*), **revenir** (*to come back*), **devenir** (*to become*), **rester** (*to stay*) , **retourner** (*to return*), **arriver** (*to arrive*), **partir** (*to leave*), **tomber** (*to fall*), **monter** (*to go up*), **descendre** (*to go down*), **entrer** (*to enter*), **sortir** (*to go out*), **naitre** (*to be born*), **mourir** (*to die*).

◆ **ÊTRE** + past participle of the verb:

Elle était   sortie.

(*She had gone out*=agrees with subject)

◆ **AVOIR** used with all other verbs

◆ **AVOIR** + past participle of the verb:

Elle a lu la poésie.

(*She read the poetry.*=no agreement with subject)

Elle l' avait lue.

(*She had read it*=agrees in gender and number with a direct object [l'=la poésie] if placed before the verb)

Verb	Past Participle
tenir (to hold)	**tenu**
lire (to read)	**lu**
voir (to see)	**vu**

Present Perfect

ai tenu (lu,vu)	**avons** tenu (lu,vu)
as tenu (lu,vu)	**avez** tenu (lu,vu)
a tenu (lu,vu)	**ont** tenu (lu,vu)

Elle a lu le journal. (*She read the newspaper.*)

Past Perfect

avais tenu (lu,vu)	**avions** tenu (lu,vu)
avais tenu (lu,vu)	**aviez** tenu (lu,vu)
avait tenu (lu,vu)	**avaient** tenu (lu,vu)

Elle avait lu le journal.
(*She has read the newspaper.*)

Past Anterior

eus tenu (lu,vu)	**eûmes** tenu (lu,vu)
eus tenu (lu,vu)	**eûtes** tenu (lu,vu)
eut tenu (lu,vu)	**eurent** tenu (lu,vu)

Elle eut lu le journal.
(*She had read the newspaper.*)

Future Perfect

aurai tenu (lu,vu)	**aurons** tenu (lu,vu)
auras tenu(lu,vu)	**aurez** tenu (lu,vu)
aura tenu(lu,vu)	**auront** tenu (lu,vu)

Elle aura lu le journal.
(*She will have read the newspaper.*)

Conditional Perfect

aurais tenu (lu,vu)	**aurions** tenu (lu,vu)
aurais tenu (lu,vu)	**auriez** tenu (lu,vu)
aurait tenu (lu,vu)	**auraient** tenu (lu,vu)

Elle aurait lu le journal.
(*She would have read the newspaper.*)

Subjunctive Perfect

aie tenu (lu,vu)	**ayons** tenu (lu,vu)
aies tenu (lu,vu)	**ayez** tenu (lu,vu)
ait tenu (lu,vu)	**aient** tenu (lu,vu)

Il faut qu' elle ait lu le journal.

(It is necessary that she has read the newspaper.)

Subjunctive Pluperfect

eusse tenu (lu,vu)	**eussions** tenu (lu,vu)
eusses tenu (lu,vu	**eussiez** tenu (lu,vu)
eût tenu (lu,vu)	**eussent** tenu (lu,vu)

Il faut qu'elle eût lu le journal.

(It is necessary that she had read the newspaper.)

Aller (*to go*)

Forms its perfect tenses with **ÊTRE**; the **past participle agrees** in gender and number with the subject:

Present Perfect

suis allé(e)	**sommes** allé(e)s
es allé(e)	**êtes** allé(e)s
est allé(e)	**sont** allé(e)s

Elle est allée au restaurant.

(She went to the restaurant.)

Past Perfect

étais allé(e)	**étions** allé(e)s
étais allé(e)	**étiez** allé(e)s
était allé(e)	**étaient** allé(e)s

Elle était allée au restaurant.

(She had gone to the restaurant.)

Past Anterior

fus allé(e)	**fûmes** allé(e)s
fus allé(e)	**fûtes** allé(e)s
fut allé(e)	**furent** allé(e)s

Elle fut allée au restaurant.

(She has gone to the restaurant.)

Future Perfect

serai allé(e)   **serons** allé(e)s
seras allé(e)   **serez** allé(e)s
sera allé(e)   **seront** allé(e)s

Elle sera allée au restaurant.

(She will have gone to the restaurant.)

Conditional Perfect

serais allé(e)   **serions** allé(e)s
serais allé(e)   **seriez** allé(e)s
serait allé(e)   **seraient** allé(e)s

Elle serait allée au restaurant.

(She would have gone to the restaurant.)

Subjunctive Perfect

sois allé(e)   **soyons** allé(e)s
sois allé(e)   **soyez** allé(e)s
soit allé(e)   **soient** allé(e)s

Il regrette que nous ne soyons pas allé(e)s en France.

(He is sorry that we didn't go to France.)

Subjunctive Pluperfect

fusse allé(e)   **fussions** allé(e)s
fusses allé(e)   **fussiez** allé(e)s
fût allé(e)   **fussent** allé(e)s

Il regrettait que nous ne fussions pas allé(e)s en France.

(He was sorry that we didn't go to France.)

Important Irregular Verbs

■ **ÊTRE -** *to be*

◆ Past Part.: **été** (conjugated with **avoir**)

◆ Present: **suis, es, est, sommes, êtes, sont**

◆ Imperfect: **étais, étais, était, étions, étiez, étaient**

◆ Simple Past: **fus, fus, fut, fûmes, fûtes, furent**

- Future: **serai, seras, sera, serons, serez, seront**
- Conditional: **serais, serais, serait, serions, seriez, seraient**
- Subj. Pres.: **sois, sois, soit, soyons, soyez, soient**
- Imperative: **sois! soyons! soyez!**

■ **AVOIR** - *to have*
- Past Part.: **eu** (conjugated with **avoir**)
- Present: **ai, as, a, avons, avez, ont**
- Imperfect: **avais, avais, avait, avions, aviez, avaient**
- Simple Past: **eus, eus, eut, eûmes, eûtes, eurent**
- Future: **aurai, auras, aura, aurons, aurez, auront**
- Conditional: **aurais, aurais, aurait, aurions, auriez, auraient**
- Subj. Pres.: **aie, aies, ait, ayons, ayez, aient**
- Imperative: **aie! ayons! ayez!**

■ Other commonly used verbs conjugated in the present tense, with the past participle and auxiliary verb given in parentheses:
- **ALLER:** *to go* (allé - être) - **vais, vas, va, allons, allez, vont**
- **BOIRE:** *to drink* (bu - avoir) - **bois, bois, boit, buvons, buvez, boivent**
- **FAIRE:** *to do, to make* (fait - avoir) - **fais, fais, fait, faisons, faites, font**
- **PRENDRE:** *to take* (pris - avoir) - **prends, prends, prend, prenons, prenez, prennent**
- **VOULOIR:** *to want* (voulu - avoir) - **veux, veux, veut, voulons, voulez, veulent**

NOTES

Mastering verbs is essential to mastering French.

"SI" Clauses

■ When the **"si"** *(if)* clause is in the present indicative, the main verb is in the present indicative, the future, or the imperative:

◆ **Si nous arrivons de bonne heure, je lui** *donne* **le cadeau** *(If we arrive early, I am giving him/her the gift)*. **Si elle arrive de bonne heure, ma mère lui** *donnera* **le cadeau** *(If she arrives early, my mother will give him/her the gift)*. **Si vous arrivez de bonne heure,** *donnez-lui* **le cadeau!** *(If you arrive early, give him/her the gift!)*

■ When the **"si"** clause is in the imperfect indicative, the main verb is in the conditional:

◆ **Si nous arrivions de bonne heure, nous lui** *donnerions* **le cadeau** *(If we arrived early, we would give him/her the gift)*.

■ When the **"si"** clause is in the pluperfect indicative, the main verb is in the conditional perfect:

◆ **Si nous étions arrivés de bonne heure, nous**

lui *aurions donné* le cadeau (*If we had arrived early, we would have given him/her the gift*).

Pronominal (Reflexive) Verbs

■ Describe daily routines and personal relationships.

■ Used where the subject and the direct (or indirect) object are the same.

    Il se rase chaque matin. (*He shaves [himself] every morning.*)

■ The following pronouns follow each subject pronoun: **me, te, se, nous, vous, se**
- ◆ **je me lave**
- ◆ **tu te laves**
- ◆ **il se lave**
- ◆ **elle se lave**
- ◆ **nous nous lavons**
- ◆ **vous vous lavez**
- ◆ **ils se lavent**
- ◆ **elles se lavent**

■ Most verbs can be used in a reflexive way:

    Il se lave (reflexive). (*He washes himself.*)

    Il lave la voiture (non-reflexive). (*He washes the car.*)

■ May be used to express two types of action:
- ◆ **Reflexive: Je me demande s'il viendra.** (*I wonder if he will come*)
- ◆ **Reciprocal: Ils se parlent tous les jours.** (*They speak to each other every day*)

■ Some verbs assume a different meaning when they become pronominal:

> *Examples:*
>   **Il ennuie les voisins.** (*He bothers the neighbors.*)
>   *vs.* **Il s'ennuie le Dimanche.** (*He is bored on Sunday.*)

- Idiomatic pronominal verbs change meaning when used in a reflexive construction.
- The verb **ÊTRE** is used as auxiliary for the compound tenses:

Non-Pronominal		Pronominal	
aller	to go	**s'en aller**	to go away
apercevoir	to see	**s'apercevoir**	to realize
attendre	to wait	**s'attendre à**	to expect
douter	to doubt	**se douter de**	to suspect
ennuyer	to bother	**s'ennuyer**	to be bored
entendre	to hear	**s'entendre avec**	to get along with
faire	to do, to make	**s'en faire**	to be worried
mettre	to put, to place	**se mettre à**	to begin
passer	to pass	**se passer de**	to do without
plaindre	to pity	**se plaindre**	to complain
servir	to serve	**se servir de**	to use
tromper	to deceive	**se tromper**	to be mistaken

Examples:
- **Ils se sont parlés.** (*They spoke to each other.*)
- **Elle s'est lavée.** (*She washed herself.*)
- **Il s'est lavé.** (*He washed himself.*)

■ When a part of the subject's body is the direct object of a reflexive verb, a definite article is used instead of a possessive adjective:
Il se lave les mains. (*He washes his hands.*)

Essential Verbs & Idiomatic Expressions
Aller (*to go*)
■ To communicate a sense of future intent
Nous allons gagner (*We will win*)
■ To feel
Comment allez-vous? *How are you?*
Je vais bien, *I feel well*; **Je vais mal**, *I feel bad*; **Je vais mieux**, *I feel better.*
■ More expressions with **ALLER**: **aller en avion**, *to go by plane*; **aller à pied**, *to go by foot*; **aller en (par) le train**, *to go by train*; **aller à bicyclette**, *to go by bicycle.*
Nous allons en voiture. (*We go by car.*)

Avoir (*to have*)
■ Helping verb used to form the perfect tenses.
■ Expresses a broad range of conditions:
avoir chaud, *to be hot*; **avoir froid**, *to be cold*; **avoir envie**, *to feel like*; **avoir faim**, *to be hungry*; **avoir soif**, *to be thirsty*; **avoir peur**, *to be fearful*; **avoir honte**, *to be ashamed*; **avoir besoin de**, *to need*; **avoir le cafard**, *to have the blues*; **avoir raison**, *to be right*; **avoir tort**, *to be wrong*; **avoir peur de**, *to be afraid*; **avoir sommeil**, *to be sleepy*; **avoir 20 ans**, *to be 20 years old*; **avoir mal**, *to have an ache*; **avoir mal à la tete**, *to have a headache*; **avoir besoin de**, *to need*; **avoir envie de**, *to want*; **avoir l'air**, *to look, to*

seem; **avoir de la chance**, *to be lucky*; **avoir de la patience**, *to be patient*; **avoir le temps**, *to have the time.*
Elle a besoin de parler avec ses amies. (*She needs to speak to her friends.*)

■ Expresses a person's age:
J'ai dix ans. (*I am 10 years old.*)

■ Expresses "there is"; "there are":
Il y a beaucoup de monde. (*There are a lot of people.*)

Examples:
• **Il y a**
  (*There is/are*)
• **Il n'y a**
  (*There is not/are not*)

Être (*to be*)

■ Expresses characteristics:
Il est grand. (*He is tall.*); **La bouteille est verte.** (*The bottle is green.*)

■ Tells the time and the date:
Il est 10 heures. (*It is 10:00.*); **C'est vendredi.** (*It is Friday.*)

■ Helping verb to form the perfect tenses of some verbs and the passive voice:
La souris est attrapée par le chat. (*The mouse is caught by the cat.*)

■ Expresses location:
Nous sommes dans le jardin. (*We are in the garden.*)

■ Expresses a condition:
Elle est heureuse. (*She is happy.*)

■ Common idiomatic expressions: **être en train de,**

to be in the act of doing something; **Je suis en train de travailler**, *I am working now*; **être égal**, *to make no difference*; **être de retour**, *to be back*.

Faire (*to do, to make*)

■ Used in the third person singular, **faire** expresses various ideas about the weather:

> **Il fait chaud**, *it is hot*; **il fait frais**, *it is cool*; **il fait froid**, *it is cold*; **il fait beau**, *the weather is nice*; **il fait mauvais**, *the weather is bad*; **il fait du soleil**, *the sun is shining*; **il fait du vent**, *it is windy*; **il fait du brouillard**, *it is foggy*; **il fait jour**, *it is daylight*; **il fait nuit**, *it is night*.

◆ Common idiomatic expressions: **faire les courses**, *to go shopping*; **faire du vélo**, *to bike*; **faire du sport**, *to play sports*; **faire les bagages**; *to pack*; **faire une promenade**, *to take a walk*; **faire un voyage**; *to take a trip*; **faire l'impossible**, *to do the impossible*; **faire de son mieux**, *to do one's best*; **faire fortune**, *to become rich*; **faire des economies**, *to save money*; **faire mal**, *to hurt*; **faire attention**, *to pay attention*; **faire peur**, *to scare*; **faire confiance**, *to trust*; **faire des courses**, *to do errands*; **faire le menage**, *to do housework*; **faire la queue**, *to wait in line*.

Elle fait une promenade le matin. (*She takes a walk in the morning.*)

Passive Voice

■ When the subject and the object are switched, use the passive voice conjugated with **ÊTRE** + past participle: The past participle agrees with the subject.

La souris est mangée par le chat.
(*The mouse is eaten by the cat.*)

As opposed to the active voice: **Le chat mange la souris.** (*The cat eats the mouse.*)

Verbs to Remember

A

■ **accepter**	to accept
■ **acheter**	to buy
■ **admirer**	to admire
■ **adorer**	to love, to adore
■ **aimer**	to like, to love
■ **aller**	to go
■ **allumer**	to turn on
■ **appeler**	to call, to name
■ **apporter**	to bring
■ **apprendre**	to learn
■ **arriver**	to arrive, to happen
■ **s'asseoir**	to sit down
■ **assister à**	to attend
■ **attendre**	to wait
■ **avoir**	to have

B

■ **baisser**	to lower
■ **boire**	to drink
■ **brosser**	to brush
■ **brûler**	to burn

C

■ **calmer**	to calm
■ **casser**	to break
■ **chanter**	to sing, to chant
■ **chauffer**	to heat (up)

■ **chercher**	to look for
■ **choisir**	to choose
■ **commencer**	to begin, to start
■ **comparer**	to compare
■ **comprendre**	to understand
■ **compter**	to count
■ **conduire**	to drive
■ **connaître**	to know someone
■ **conseiller**	to advise
■ **continuer**	to continue
■ **couper**	to cut
■ **courir**	to run
■ **crier**	to yell
■ **croire**	to believe

D

■ **danser**	to dance
■ **décrire**	to describe
■ **demander**	to ask
■ **descendre**	to go down, to descend
■ **désirer**	to desire, to want, to wish
■ **désobéir (à)**	to disobey
■ **dessiner**	to draw
■ **détester**	to detest
■ **détruire**	to destroy
■ **devenir**	to become
■ **devoir**	to have to (must), to owe
■ **dire**	to say, to tell
■ **diriger**	to manage, to lead, to direct
■ **disparaître**	to disappear
■ **divorcer**	to divorce
■ **donner**	to give
■ **dormir**	to sleep

E

économiser	to save
écouter	to listen
écrire	to write
effacer	to erase
embrasser	to kiss
employer	to use, to employ
emprunter	to borrow
s'endormir	to fall asleep
s'ennuyer	to be bored
entrer	to come in, to enter
envoyer	to send
épeler	to spell
espérer	to hope
espionner	to spy
s'essuyer	to dry off, to wipe
éteindre	to turn off
être	to be
étudier	to study
examiner	to examine
exiger	to demand, to require
expliquer	to explain

F

faire	to do, to make
faire mal	to hurt
falloir	to have to, to need to
finir	to finish
fonctionner	to work, to operate, to function

G

gaspiller	to waste
geler	to freeze
goûter	to taste, to sample, to try
grandir	to grow up
grossir	to gain weight

H

habiter	to reside

I

identifier	to identify
imaginer	to dream up, to imagine
s'inquiéter	to worry
intruire	to educate
inventer	to dream up, to invent
inviter	to invite

J

jeter	to throw
joindre	to join
jouer	to play
juger	to judge, to try (in court)

L

laver	to wash
lever	to get up
lire	to read
louer	to rent

M

■ **maigrir**	to lose weight
■ **manger**	to eat
■ **marcher**	to walk
■ **marier**	to marry, to join
■ **marquer**	to mark
■ **mélanger**	to mix
■ **menacer**	to threaten
■ **mettre**	to put
■ **monter**	to go up, to ascend
■ **montrer**	to show
■ **mourir**	to die

N

■ **nager**	to swim
■ **naître**	to be born
■ **noter**	to note

O

■ **obéir (à)**	to obey
■ **observer**	to observe
■ **obtenir**	to obtain
■ **offrir**	to offer
■ **oublier**	to forget
■ **ouvrir**	to open

P

■ **parler**	to speak, to talk
■ **partager**	to share
■ **partir**	to leave
■ **passer**	to pass by, to come by

■ **payer**	to pay
■ **peigner**	to comb
■ **peindre**	to paint
■ **penser**	to think
■ **perdre**	to lose
■ **permettre**	to allow, to permit
■ **pleurer**	to cry
■ **pleuvoir**	to rain
■ **polluer**	to pollute
■ **porter**	to wear
■ **pousser**	to push
■ **pouvoir**	to be able to
■ **préférer**	to prefer
■ **prendre**	to take
■ **préparer**	to prepare
■ **présenter**	to present
■ **prêter**	to lend
■ **prier (pour)**	to pray (over/for)
■ **produire**	to produce
■ **(se) promener**	to take a walk, to walk around
■ **promettre**	to promise
■ **punir**	to punish

Q
■ **quitter**	to leave

R
■ **raconter**	to tell (a tale), to relate (a story), to narrate
■ **(se) rappeler**	to remember
■ **(se) raser**	to shave

■ **reconnaître**	to recognize
■ **réfléchir**	to dream up
■ **refuser**	to refuse
■ **regarder**	to look at, to watch
■ **regretter**	to regret
■ **remarquer**	to notice
■ **remplir**	to fill
■ **rencontrer**	to meet
■ **rendre**	to give back
■ **renseigner**	to inform
■ **répéter**	to repeat
■ **répondre**	to answer, to respond
■ **(se) reposer**	to rest
■ **réserver**	to reserve
■ **respirer**	to breathe
■ **rester**	to stay
■ **retourner**	to go back, to return
■ **réussir (à)**	to succeed
■ **(se) réveiller**	to wake (up), to arise
■ **rêver de**	to dream of
■ **revenir**	to come back
■ **rire**	to laugh
■ **rougir**	to blush
■ **rouler**	to roll

S

■ **savoir**	to know something
■ **sembler**	to seem
■ **séparer**	to separate
■ **servir**	to serve
■ **soigner**	to take care of
■ **sortir**	to go out
■ **souhaiter**	to wish (something) for (someone)

■ **sourire**	to smile
■ **se souvenir (de)**	to remember
■ **suggérer**	to suggest
■ **suivre**	to follow

T

■ **tâcher**	to try
■ **téléphoner**	to phone
■ **tenter**	to try, to attempt
■ **tomber**	to fall
■ **toucher**	to touch
■ **tourner**	to turn
■ **tousser**	to cough
■ **tracer**	to trace
■ **travailler**	to work
■ **trier**	to sort
■ **(se) tromper**	to be mistaken

U

■ **unifier**	to unify
■ **unir**	to unite, to join
■ **utiliser**	to use, to utilize

V

■ **vendre**	to sell
■ **venir**	to come
■ **vérifier**	to check, to verify
■ **visiter**	to visit
■ **voler**	to fly, to steal
■ **vouloir**	to want, to hope for
■ **voyager**	to travel

NOTES
Measurements = **Les Mesures**

- centimeter — **le centimètre** (0.39 in.)
- meter — **le mètre** (3.28 feet)
- kilometer — **le kilomètre** (0.621 mile)
- liter — **le litre** (1.75 pints)
- gram — **le gramme** (0.0352 oz.)
- kilogram — **le kilo(gramme)** (2.20 lbs)

Clothes

16

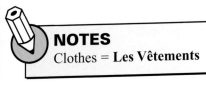

NOTES
Clothes = **Les Vêtements**

Examples:
- "It looks good on you!"
  "Ça vous va bien!"
- "What's your size?"
  "Quelle est votre taille?"

Add (-s) for plurals; irregular plurals are listed

bag	**le sac**
bathing suit	**le maillot de bain**
belt	**la ceinture**
blouse	**le chemisier**
boots	**les bottes (f.)**
bra	**le soutien-gorge**
cap	**la casquette**
cheap	**bon marché**
coat	**le manteau/x**
cotton	**le coton**
dress	**la robe**
expensive	**cher/ère**

■ glove	**le gant**
■ handbag	**le sac à main**
■ hat	**le chapeau/x**
■ jacket	**la veste**
■ jeans	**le jean**
■ lace	**la dentelle**
■ leather	**le cuir**
■ nightgown	**la chemise de nuit**
■ pants	**le pantalon**
■ panty hose	**le collant**
■ pajamas	**le pyjama**
■ rain coat	**l'imperméable(m)**
■ sandal	**la sandale**
■ scarf	**le foulard**
■ shirt	**la chemise**
■ shoe	**la chaussure**
■ shorts	**le short**
■ silk	**la soie**
■ size	**la taille**
■ skirt	**la jupe**
■ sleeve	**la manche**
■ sock	**la chaussette**
■ suit (man's)	**le complet**
■ suit (woman's)	**le tailleur**
■ sweater	**le pull(over)**
■ swim suit	**le maillot (de bain)**
■ T-shirt	**le tee-shirt**
■ tennis shoes	**les tennis**
■ tie	**la cravate**
■ umbrella	**le parapluie**
■ underwear	**le sous-vêtement**
■ wallet	**le portefeuille**
■ wool	**la laine**

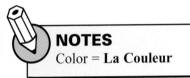

NOTES
Color = **La Couleur**

- beige   **beige**
- black   **noir/e**
- blue   **bleu/e**
- brown   **marron**
- green   **vert/e**
- grey   **gris/e**
- orange   **orange**
- pink   **rose**
- purple   **violet/te**
- red   **rouge**
- yellow   **jaune**
- white   **blanc/-che**

- dark   **foncé/e**
- light   **clair/e**

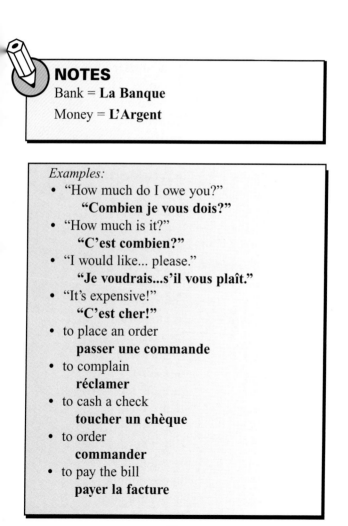

NOTES

Bank = **La Banque**

Money = **L'Argent**

Examples:

- "How much do I owe you?"
  "Combien je vous dois?"
- "How much is it?"
  "C'est combien?"
- "I would like... please."
  "Je voudrais...s'il vous plaît."
- "It's expensive!"
  "C'est cher!"
- to place an order
  passer une commande
- to complain
  réclamer
- to cash a check
  toucher un chèque
- to order
  commander
- to pay the bill
  payer la facture

Add (-s) for plurals; irregular plurals are listed

■ account	**le compte**
■ balance	**le solde**
■ bank	**la banque**
■ bank account	**le compte bancaire**
■ bill	**la facture**
■ business trip	**le voyage d'affaires**
■ calendar	**le calendrier**
■ cash	**les espèces (f.)**
■ cash register	**la caisse**
■ to change	**changer**
■ to clear up	**clarifier**
■ complaint	**la réclamation**
■ credit card	**la carte de crédit**
■ customer	**le client**
■ customs	**la douane**
■ customs officer	**le douanier**
■ delivery	**la livraison**
■ department store	**le grand magasin**
■ dollar	**le dollar**
■ to endorse	**endosser**
■ exchange bureau	**le bureau de change**
■ expenses	**les frais/dépenses**
■ interest	**le taux d'intérêt**
■ in writing	**par écrit**
■ mail box	**la boîte aux lettres**
■ manager	**le directeur**
■ maturity date	**l'échéance (f.)**
■ money	**l'argent (m.)**
■ money order	**le mandat**
■ order	**la commande**
■ payee	**le bénéficiaire**

■ payment	**le paiement**
■ percentage	**le pourcentage**
■ personal check	**le chèque personnel**
■ phone book	**l'annuaire (m.)**
■ P.O. box	**la boîte postale**
■ postage	**l'affranchissement (m.)**
■ postage stamp	**le timbre-poste**
■ post office	**la poste**
■ price	**le prix**
■ price (net)	**le prix net**
■ publicity	**la publicité**
■ rate	**le cours**
■ receipt	**le reçu**
■ refund	**le remboursement**
■ to refund	**rembourser**
■ registered mail	**la lettre recommandée**
■ salary	**le salaire**
■ sale	**les soldes (f.)**
■ salesclerk	**le vendeur/la vendeuse**
■ sales department	**le service de vente**
■ to save money	**économiser de l'argent**
■ savings	**les économies (f.)**
■ to sell	**vendre**
■ shipment	**l'expédition (f.)**
■ small change	**la petite monnaie**
■ spendings	**les dépenses (f.)**
■ stock	**le stock**
■ to tax	**taxer**
■ telegram	**le télégramme**
■ teller	**le caissier**
■ terms of delivery	**les conditions de livraison**
■ terms of payments	**les conditions de paiement**
■ trade	**le commerce**

■ transfer	**le virement**
■ to transfer money	**virer de l'argent**
■ transfer slip	**l'avis de virement (m.)**
■ traveler's check	**le chèque de voyage**
■ valid	**valide**
■ value	**la valeur**
■ wallet	**le portefeuille**
■ wire	**le télégramme**
■ to wire	**télégraphier**
■ withdrawal	**le retrait**

NOTES
Greetings = **Les Salutations**

■ hello, Mr.	**bonjour, monsieur**
■ hello, Mrs.	**bonjour, madame**
■ hello, Ms./Miss	**bonjour, mademoiselle**
■ hello	**bonjour**
■ hi	**salut**

Examples:

- "How are you?"
  "Comment allez-vous?"
- "What's your name?"
  "Comment vous appelez-vous?"
- "My name is... "
  "Je m'appelle..."
- "I introduce...to you"
  "Je vous présente..."
- "Speak slowly please."
  "Parlez lentement s'il vous plaît."

delighted	**enchanté/e**
fine	**ça va bien**
good-bye	**au revoir/salut**
good evening	**bonsoir**
good night	**bonne nuit**
many thanks	**merci beaucoup**
not at all	**de rien**
not bad	**pas mal**
please	**s'il vous plaît**
see you soon	**à bientôt**
thank you	**merci**
very well	**très bien**
what?	**comment?/quoi?**
you are welcome	**je vous (t')en prie**

Travel / Directions

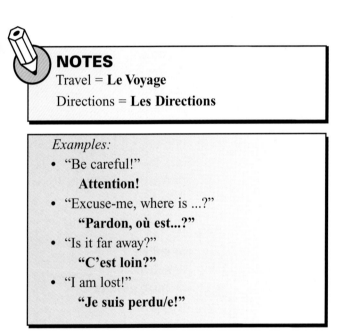

NOTES

Travel = **Le Voyage**

Directions = **Les Directions**

Examples:
- "Be careful!"
  Attention!
- "Excuse-me, where is ...?"
  "Pardon, où est...?"
- "Is it far away?"
  "C'est loin?"
- "I am lost!"
  "Je suis perdu/e!"

Add (-s) for plurals; irregular plurals are listed

Travel

■ address book	**le carnet d'adresses**
■ airport	**l'aéroport (m.)**
■ bicycle	**le vélo**
■ boat	**le bateau(x)**
■ bus (city)	**le bus**
■ bus (excursion)	**le car**

■ camera	**l'appareil-photo (m.)**
■ car	**la voiture**
■ cash	**en espèces**
■ credit card	**la carte de crédit**
■ euro (money)	**l'euro (m.)**
■ exit	**la sortie**
■ film (a roll)	**la pellicule**
■ flight	**le vol**
■ guide	**le guide**
■ highway	**l'autoroute (f.)**
■ map	**la carte**
■ money, change	**la monnaie**
■ moped	**la mobylette**
■ motorcycle	**la moto**
■ to park	**(se) garer**
■ parking lot	**parc de stationnement**
■ passerby	**le/la passante**
■ passport	**le passeport**
■ plane	**l'avion (m.)**
■ police	**la police**
■ policeman	**le policier**
■ postcard	**la carte postale**
■ public	**le public**
■ reservation	**la réservation**
■ road	**la route**
■ stop	**l'arrêt**
■ stoplight	**le feu rouge**
■ subway	**le métro**
■ sunglasses	**les lunettes (f.) de soleil**
■ taxi	**le taxi**
■ tourism	**le tourisme**
■ tourist	**la/le touriste**
■ town hall	**la mairie**

■ traffic circle	**le rond-point**
■ train	**le train**
■ transportation	**les transports en commun**
■ train station	**la gare**
■ travel agency	**l'agence de voyages (f.)**
■ U-turn	**le demi-tour**
■ vacations	**les vacances**

Directions

■ above, on	**en haut/sur**
■ at the home of/ at the place of	**chez**
■ behind	**derrière**
■ below, under	**en bas/sous**
■ between	**entre**
■ facing	**en face**
■ far	**loin de**
■ here	**ici**
■ in front of	**devant**
■ inside	**dedans**
■ near	**près de**
■ next to	**à côté de**
■ outside	**dehors**
■ straight ahead	**tout droit**
■ there	**là**
■ (to the) left	**(à) gauche**
■ (to the) right	**(à) droite**
■ with	**avec**
■ without	**sans**

Directions

■ north	**le nord**
■ south	**le sud**
■ west	**l'ouest**
■ east	**l'est**
■ southwest	**le sud-ouest**
■ northeast	**le nord-est**

21 Months, Seasons & Days of the Week

Months

- January   **janvier**
- February   **février**
- March   **mars**
- April   **avril**
- May   **mai**
- June   **juin**
- July   **juillet**
- August   **août**
- September   **septembre**
- October   **octobre**
- November   **novembre**
- December   **décembre**

Seasons

- spring   **le printemps**
- summer   **l'été (m.)**
- fall   **l'automne (m.)**
- winter   **l'hiver (m.)**

Days of the Week

Examples:
- "What day is it?"
  "Quel jour sommes-nous?"

- "Today is July 14, 2006."
  "Aujourd'hui, c'est le 14 juillet 2006."

■ Monday	**lundi**
■ Tuesday	**mardi**
■ Wednesday	**mercredi**
■ Thursday	**jeudi**
■ Friday	**vendredi**
■ Saturday	**samedi**
■ Sunday	**dimanche**
■ weekend	**le weekend**

Time / When

NOTES
Time = **L'Heure**
When = **Quand**

Examples:
- "What time is it?"
  "Quelle heure est-il?"
- "It is a quarter of 2."
  "Il est 2 heures moins le quart."

Time

■ 1 A.M.	**une heure du matin**
■ 1:05	**une heure cinq**
■ 2:10	**deux heures dix**
■ 3:15	**trois heures et quart**
■ 4:30	**quatre heures et demie**
■ 5:35	**six heures moins vingt-cinq**
■ 11:45 A.M.	**onze heures quarante cinq**
	or midi moins le quart
■ noon	**midi**
■ midnight	**minuit**

When

■ a long time ago	**il y a longtemps**
■ afternoon	**l'après-midi (m.)**
■ ago; there is/are	**il y a**
■ an hour ago	**il y a une heure**
■ at that moment	**à ce moment-là**
■ evening	**le soir/la soirée**
■ morning	**le matin**
■ next month	**le mois prochain**
■ next summer	**l'été prochain (m.)**
■ next year	**l'année prochaine (f.)**
■ night	**la nuit**
■ not so long ago	**il n'y a pas longtemps**
■ soon	**bientôt**
■ that day	**ce jour-là**
■ the day after tomororrow	**après-demain**
■ the day before yesterday	**avant-hier**
■ this weekend	**ce week-end**
■ today	**aujourd'hui**
■ tomorrow	**demain**
■ tonight	**ce soir**
■ yesterday	**hier**

NOTES
Weather = **Le Temps**
Climate = **Le Climat**

Examples:

- "How's the weather?"
  "Quel temps fait-il?"
- "What's the temperature outside?"
  "Quelle est la température dehors?"
- "It's 20 degrees this morning."
  "Il fait 20 degrés ce matin."
- "What's the weather like?"
  "Quel temps fait-il?"

■ cloud	**le nuage**
■ cold	**le froid**
■ frost	**le gel**
■ hail	**la grêle**
■ heat	**la chaleur**
■ humidity	**l'humidité (f.)**
■ ice	**la glace**
■ inside	**dedans**
■ it's a full moon	**c'est la pleine lune**
■ it's bad weather	**il fait mauvais**

■ it's beautiful	**il fait beau**
■ it's cloudy	**il y a des nuages**
■ it's cold	**il fait froid**
■ it's cool	**il fait frais**
■ it's foggy	**il fait du brouillard**
■ it's freezing	**il gèle**
■ it's hot	**il fait chaud**
■ it's humid	**il fait humide**
■ it's nice	**il fait bon**
■ it's overcast	**le ciel est couvert**
■ it's raining	**il pleut**
■ it's snowing	**il neige**
■ it's stormy	**il y a de l'orage**
■ it's sunny	**il fait du soleil**
■ it's warm	**il fait chaud**
■ it's windy	**il fait du vent**
■ lightning	**l'éclair (m.)**
■ moon	**la lune**
■ outside	**dehors**
■ rain	**la pluie**
■ sky	**le ciel**
■ snow	**la neige**
■ storm	**l'orage (m.)**
■ sun	**le soleil**
■ thunder	**le tonnerre**
■ wind	**le vent**

NOTES
Habitat = **L'Habitation**

Examples:
- "Where do you live?"
  "Où habitez-vous?"

Add (-s) for plurals; irregular plurals are listed

■ agency	**l'agence (f.)**
■ apartment	**l'appartement (m.)**
■ armchair	**le fauteuil**
■ artist studio	**l'atelier (m.)**
■ balcony	**le balcon**
■ bathroom	**la salle de bain**
■ bathroom sink	**le lavabo**
■ bathtub	**la baignoire**
■ bed	**le lit**
■ bedroom	**la chambre à coucher**
■ bedsheet	**le drap**
■ bedside table	**la table de nuit**
■ blanket	**la couverture**
■ bookshelf	**l'étagère (f.)**
■ building	**l'immeuble (m.)**
■ calculator	**la calculatrice**

101

■ chair	**la chaise**
■ city	**la ville**
■ clock (alarm)	**le réveil**
■ closet	**le placard**
■ compact disk	**le CD**
■ computer	**l'ordinateur (m.)**
■ courtyard	**la cour**
■ cupboard	**le placard**
■ curtain	**le rideau**
■ desk	**le bureau/x**
■ dining room	**la salle à manger**
■ door	**la porte**
■ dormitory	**la résidence universitaire**
■ downtown	**le centre-ville**
■ drinkable water	**l'eau potable (f.)**
■ electricity	**l'électricité (f.)**
■ elevator	**l'ascenseur (m.)**
■ entrance	**l'entrée (f.)**
■ first floor	**le rez de chaussée**
■ floor	**l'étage (m.)**
■ furniture	**les meubles**
■ garage	**le garage**
■ gas (cooking)	**le gaz**
■ hallway	**le couloir**
■ heating (central)	**le chauffage (central)**
■ high school	**le lycée**
■ hotel	**l'hôtel (m.)**
■ hot plate	**le réchaud**
■ house	**la maison**
■ kitchen	**la cuisine**
■ lamp	**la lampe**
■ landlord/landlady	**le/la propriétaire**
■ living room	**la salle de séjour**

mattress	**le matelas**
mirror	**la glace**
neighborhood	**le quartier**
photograph	**la photo**
pillow	**l'oreiller (m.)**
plant	**la plante**
poster	**l'affiche (f.)**
radiator	**le radiateur**
real estate	**l'immobilier**
real estate agency	**l'agence immobilière (f.)**
recycling	**le recyclage**
refrigerator	**le frigidaire**
rent	**le loyer**
to rent	**louer**
room	**la pièce**
rug	**le tapis**
shower	**la douche**
smoke	**la fumée**
sofa	**le sofa**
staircase	**l'escalier (m.)**
stereo system	**la chaîne stéréo**
street	**la rue**
studio apartment	**le studio**
suburb	**la banlieue**
telephone	**le téléphone**
television	**la télé(vision)**
terrace	**la terrasse**
toilet	**le W.C.**
towel	**la serviette**
wall	**le mur**
wastebasket	**la corbeille**

25 The Family / People

Add (-s) for plurals; irregular plurals are listed

Family

■ aunt	**la tante**
■ best friend	**le/la meilleur/e ami/e**
■ brother	**le frère**
■ child	**l'enfant**
■ cousin	**le/la cousin/e**
■ daughter	**la fille**
■ father	**le père**
■ friend	**l'ami/e**
■ grandchild	**le petit-enfant**
■ granddaughter	**la petite-fille**
■ grandfather	**le grand-père**
■ grandmother	**la grand-mère**
■ grandparent	**le grand-parent**
■ grandson	**le petit-fils**
■ husband	**le mari**
■ mother	**la mère**
■ nephew	**le neveu/x**

■ niece	**la nièce**
■ parents/relatives	**les parents**
■ sister	**la soeur**
■ son	**le fils**
■ stepfather/ father-in-law	**le beau-père**
■ stepmother/ mother-in-law	**la belle-mère**
■ twin	**le jumeau/x-jumelle/s**
■ uncle	**l'oncle**
■ wife/woman	**la femme**

People

> *Examples:*
> • "What's your name?"
>   **"Comment vous appelez-vous?"**

■ Mr.	**Monsieur**
■ Mrs.	**Madame**
■ Ms./Miss.	**Mademoiselle**
■ honeymoon	**la lune de miel**
■ love at first sight	**le coup de foudre**
■ to be in love	**être amoureux/-se**
■ to fall in love	**tomber amoureux/-se**
■ to like	**aimer, aimer bien**
■ to love	**aimer**

26

The Body / Health

NOTES
The Body = **Le Corps**
Health = **La Santé**

Examples:

- "Where does it hurt?"
  "Où avez-vous mal?"
- "I feel sick."
  "Je me sens mal."
- "I feel great!"
  "Je me sens bien/je suis en forme!"
- "You look sick."
  "Vous avez l'air malade."
- "Rest!"
  "Reposez-vous!"
- "It burns!"
  "Ça brûle!"

■ to be cold	**avoir froid**
■ to be hot	**avoir chaud**
■ to be hungry	**avoir faim**
■ to be thirsty	**avoir soif**
■ to be 20 years old	**avoir vingt ans**
■ to be sleepy	**avoir sommeil**

to get a sunburn	**attraper un coup de soleil**
to have a headache	**avoir mal à la tête**
to have a stomachache	**avoir mal au ventre**
to have a toothache	**avoir mal aux dents**
to hurt	**avoir mal**
to sprain	**(se) fouler**

Add (-s) for plurals; irregular plurals are listed

Body

ankle	**la cheville**
arm	**le bras**
back	**le dos**
belly	**le ventre**
chest	**la poitrine**
ear	**l'oreille (f.)**
eye(s)	**l'oeil/les yeux (m.)**
eyebrow	**le sourcil**
face	**le visage**
finger	**le doigt**
foot	**le pied**
hair	**les cheveux (m.)**
hand	**la main**
head	**la tête**
heart	**le coeur**
knee	**le genou/x**
leg	**la jambe**
lip	**la lèvre**
liver	**le foie**
lung	**le poumon**
mouth	**la bouche**
neck	**le cou**

- nose   **le nez**
- shoulder   **l'épaule (f.)**
- stomach   **l'estomac (m.)**
- throat   **la gorge**
- toe   **le doigt de pied**
- tooth   **la dent**
- wrist   **le poignet**

Health

- antibiotic   **l'antibiotique (m.)**
- antiseptic   **l'antiseptique (m.)**
- aspirin   **l'aspirine (f.)**
- blood   **le sang**
- bronchitis   **la bronchite**
- burn   **la brûlure**
- cast   **le plâtre**
- cold   **le rhume**
- cough   **la toux**
- cough syrup   **le sirop pour la toux**
- death   **la mort**
- diagnosis   **le diagnostic**
- diet   **le régime**
- doctor   **le medecin/le docteur**
- drop   **la goutte**
- fever   **la fièvre**
- flu   **la grippe**
- herbal tea   **la tisane**
- illness   **la maladie**
- indigestion   **l'indigestion (f.)**
- infection   **l'infection (f.)**
- injection   **la piqûre**
- medicine (drugs) **le médicament**
- nausea   **la nausée, le mal au coeur**

■ ointment	**la pommade**
■ pain	**la douleur**
■ patient	**le/la malade**
■ penicillin	**la pénicilline**
■ pharmacy	**la pharmacie**
■ prescription	**l'ordonnance (f.)**
■ remedy	**le remède**
■ shot	**la piqûre**
■ sickness	**la maladie**
■ sore throat	**le mal de gorge**
■ sunburn	**le coup de soleil**
■ swollen	**enflé/e**
■ syrup	**le sirop**
■ temperature	**la température**
■ thermometer	**le thermomètre**
■ toothache	**le mal au dent**

Studies & the Workplace

NOTES
Studies = **Les Études**
Workplace = **Le Travail**

Examples:
- "Study!"
  "Etudiez!"
- "Work!"
  "Travaillez!"
- To do a degree in French
  Préparer un diplôme en français
- To earn money
  Gagner de l'argent
- To study
  Etudier
- To take a course
  Suivre un cours

Add (-s) for plurals; irregular plurals are listed

■ accountant	**le/la comptable**
■ accounting	**la comptabilité**
■ actor/actress	**l'acteur/l'actrice**
■ advertising	**la publicité (la pub)**
■ anthropology	**l'anthropologie (f.)**
■ architect	**l'architecte**

■ the arts	**les arts (m.)**
■ astronomy	**l'astronomie (f.)**
■ atlas	**l'atlas (m.)**
■ B.A/B.S degree	**le baccalauréat**
■ biography	**la biographie**
■ biology	**la biologie**
■ book	**le livre**
■ bookstore	**la librairie**
■ botany	**la botanique**
■ business studies	**les études commerciales (f.)**
■ campus	**le campus**
■ career	**la carrière**
■ chemistry	**la chimie**
■ colleague	**le/la collègue**
■ college	**la faculté**
■ computer	**l'ordinateur**
■ computer science	**l'informatique (f.)**
■ course	**le cours**
■ degree	**le diplôme**
■ dentist	**le/la dentiste**
■ dictionary	**le dictionnaire**
■ doctor	**le docteur/le médecin**
■ economics	**les sciences (f.) économiques**
■ education	**l'éducation (f.)**
■ encyclopedia	**l'encyclopédie (f.)**
■ engineer	**l'ingénieur/e**
■ enrollment	**l'inscription (f.)**
■ exam	**l'examen (m.)**
■ factory	**l'usine (f.)**
■ fine arts	**les beaux-arts**
■ foreign languages	**les langues étrangères**
■ geography	**la géographie**
■ geology	**la géologie**

■ grade	la note
■ gymnasium	le gymnase
■ health clinic	l'infirmerie (f.)
■ history	l'histoire (f.)
■ hospital	l'hôpital/aux (m.)
■ humanities	les sciences (f.) humaines
■ job	l'emploi (m.)
■ journalism	le journalisme
■ journalist	le/la journaliste
■ laboratory	le laboratoire
■ language lab	le labo de langues
■ law	le droit
■ law school	la faculté (la fac) de droit
■ lawyer	l'avocat/e
■ lecture hall	l'amphithéâtre (m.)
■ liberal arts	les lettres (f.)
■ library	la bibliothèque
■ linguistics	la linguistique
■ literature	la littérature
■ magazine	le magazine
■ major	la spécialisation
■ mathematics	les mathématiques (les maths)
■ mechanic	le/la mécanicien/ne
■ medicine	la médecine
■ money	l'argent (m.)
■ music	la musique
■ musician	le/la musicien/ne
■ natural sciences	les sciences (f.) naturelles
■ newspaper	le journal/-aux
■ nurse	l'infirmier/-ère
■ office	le bureau/x
■ painter	le peintre

painting	**la peinture**
pharmacist	**le pharmacien/ne**
philosophy	**la philosophie**
physics	**la physique**
physiology	**la physiologie**
playing field	**le terrain de sport**
police officer	**l'agent de police**
political sciences	**les sciences politiques**
press	**la presse**
professor	**le professeur (le prof)**
psychology	**la psychologie**
report	**le rapport**
schedule	**l'emploi du temps (m.)**
school	**l'école (f.)**
secretary	**le/la secrétaire**
semester	**le semestre**
singer	**le chanteur/-euse**
snack bar	**le snack-bar**
social worker	**l'assistant/e social/e**
sociology	**la sociologie**
stadium	**le stade**
studies	**les études (f.)**
teacher (elementary)	**l'instituteur/-trice**
technician	**le/la technicien/-ne**
theater	**le théâtre**
trimester	**le trimestre**
waiter/waitress	**le serveur/la serveuse**
work	**le travail/aux**
(full-time) work	**le travail/aux à plein temps**
(part-time) work	**le travail à mi-temps**
writer	**l'écrivain**
zoology	**la zoologie**

NOTES
Computer = **L'Ordinateur**

- CD-ROM drive — **le CD-ROM**
- computer file — **le fichier**
- database — **la banque de données**
- electronic mail — **le courrier électronique**
- floppy disk — **la disquette**
- hard drive — **le disque dur**
- keyboard — **le clavier**
- laptop — **le portable**
- monitor — **le moniteur**
- mouse — **la souris**
- network — **le réseau/x**
- printer — **l'imprimante (f.)**
- program — **le logiciel**
- save — **sauvegarder**
- screen — **l'écran (m.)**
- technology — **la technologie**
- wordprocessing — **le traitement de texte**

29 Sports & Entertainment

Examples:
- "I am having fun!"
  "Je m'amuse bien!"
- "I love vacations!"
  "J'adore les vacances!"

■ to exercise	**faire de l'exercice (m.)**
■ to go camping	**faire du camping**
■ to go fishing	**aller à la pêche**
■ to go horseback riding	**faire du cheval**
■ to go jogging	**faire du jogging**
■ to go mountain climbing	**faire de l'alpinisme**
■ to go on vacation	**partir en vacances**
■ to go sailing	**faire de la voile**
■ to go to a concert	**aller à un concert**
■ to go to the beach	**aller à la plage**
■ to perform a play	**jouer une pièce**
■ to play dominos	**jouer aux dominos**
■ to play rugby	**jouer au rugby**
■ to read the paper	**lire le journal**

■ to ride a bike   **faire du vélo**
■ to run   **courir**
■ to see an exhibition **voir une exposition**
■ to (ice) skate   **faire du patinage**
                        (à glace)
■ to (water) ski   **faire du ski (nautique)**
■ to spend a quiet evening **passer une soirée**
                        tranquille
■ to swim   **nager (la natation)**
■ to take a hike   **faire une randonnée**
■ to take a walk   **faire une promenade**
■ to walk   **marcher**
■ to windsurf   **faire de la planche**
                        à voile

Add (-s) for plurals; irregular plurals are listed
■ basketball   **le basketball (le basket)**
■ broadcast (program)   **l'émission (f.)**
■ camping   **le camping**
■ cards   **les cartes (f.)**
■ cartoon   **le dessin animé**
■ checkers   **les dames**
■ chess   **les échecs**
■ comedy   **la comédie**
■ concert   **le concert**
■ documentary   **le documentaire**
■ game   **le jeu/x**
■ golf   **le golf**
■ guitar   **la guitare**
■ jazz   **le jazz**
■ mountain bike   **le VTT(vélo-**
                        tout-terrain)
■ mountain climbing   **l'alpinisme**

■ movie	**le film**
■ movie star	**la vedette**
■ movie theater	**le cinéma**
■ museum	**le musée**
■ music	**la musique**
■ news	**les nouvelles**
■ party	**la fête**
■ piano	**le piano**
■ place	**l'endroit (m.)**
■ play	**la pièce de théâtre**
■ race	**la course**
■ radio	**la radio**
■ remote control	**la télécommande**
■ rest	**le repos**
■ rugby	**le rugby**
■ seat	**la place**
■ screen	**l'écran (m.)**
■ show	**le spectacle**
■ soap opera	**le feuilleton**
■ soccer	**le football (le foot)**
■ sport	**le sport**
■ swimming pool	**la piscine**
■ tape recorder	**le magnétophone**
■ television	**la télévision (la télé)**
■ tennis	**le tennis**
■ theater	**le théâtre**
■ ticket	**le billet**
■ TV station	**la chaîne de télé**

30 Food & Restaurant

NOTES
Food = **La Nourriture**
Restaurant = **Le Restaurant**

Examples:

- "I would like...."
  "Je voudrais..."
- "I would like to order, please."
  "Je voudrais commander, s'il vous plaît."
- "The check please!"
  "L'addition? s'il vous plaît!"
- "The service is included?"
  "Le service est compris?"

Desserts

■ cake	**le gâteau/x**
■ chocolate	**le chocolat**
■ cookie	**le biscuit**
■ cream	**la crème**
■ crepe	**la crêpe**
■ doughnut	**le beignet**
■ ice cream	**la glace**
■ tart	**la tarte**

Drinks

■ beer	**la bière**
■ bottle	**la bouteille**
■ beer (light)	**la bière légère**
■ beer (dark)	**la bière brune**
■ cola	**le coca(-cola)**
■ Coke (diet)	**coca light**
■ coffee	**le café**
■ hot chocolate	**le chocolat chaud**
■ ice	**la glace**
■ lemonade	**la citronnade**
■ milk	**le lait**
■ orange juice	**le jus d'orange**
■ tea	**le thé**
■ water (iced)	**l'eau (glacée) (f.)**
■ wine	**le vin**
■ wine (red)	**le vin rouge**
■ wine (rose)	**le vin rosé**
■ wine (white)	**le vin blanc**

Fish

■ lobster	**le homard**
■ salmon	**le saumon**
■ shrimp	**la crevette**
■ sole	**la sole**
■ tuna	**le thon**
■ trout	**la truite**

Fruits

■ apple	**la pomme**
■ apricot	**l'abricot (m.)**
■ avocado	**l'avocat (m.)**
■ banana	**la banane**
■ cherry	**la cerise**

■ grapefruit	**le pamplemousse**
■ grapes	**le raisin**
■ lemon	**le citron**
■ mango	**la mangue**
■ olive	**l'olive (f.)**
■ orange	**l'orange (f.)**
■ pear	**la poire**
■ raspberry	**la framboise**
■ strawberry	**la fraise**

Meal

Add (-s) for plurals; irregular plurals are listed

■ appetizer	**l'entrée (f.)**
■ bread	**le pain**
■ breakfast	**le petit déjeuner**
■ butter	**le beurre**
■ cake	**le gâteau/x**
■ candy	**le bonbon**
■ cheese	**le fromage**
■ chocolate	**le chocolat**
■ cup	**la tasse**
■ egg	**l'oeuf (m.)**
■ fork	**la fourchette**
■ french fries	**les frites (f.)**
■ glass	**le verre**
■ hamburger	**le hamburger**
■ knife	**le couteau/x**
■ lunch	**le déjeuner**
■ meal	**le repas**
■ mustard	**la moutarde**
■ napkin	**la serviette**
■ oil	**l'huile (f.)**
■ pasta	**les pâtes (f.)**

■ pepper	**le poivre**
■ pizza	**la pizza**
■ rice	**le riz**
■ salt	**le sel**
■ sandwich	**le sandwich**
■ snack	**le casse-croûte/snack**
■ snail	**l'escargot (m.)**
■ spices	**les épices (f.)**
■ tip	**le pourboire**
■ vinegar	**le vinaigre**

Meat

■ beef	**le boeuf**
■ chicken	**le poulet**
■ chop	**la côtelette**
■ deli	**la charcuterie**
■ goose	**l'oie (f.)**
■ gravy	**la sauce**
■ ham	**le jambon**
■ rabbit	**le lapin**
■ turkey	**la dinde**
■ veal	**le veau**

Vegetables

■ beet	**la betterave**
■ broccoli	**le broccoli**
■ cabbage	**le chou**
■ carrot	**la carotte**
■ celery	**le céleri**
■ chestnut	**le marron**
■ corn	**le maïs**
■ cucumber	**le concombre**
■ eggplant	**l'aubergine (f.)**
■ endive	**l'endive (f.)**

- green bean — **le haricot vert (m.)**
- lettuce — **la laitue**
- mushroom — **le champignon**
- onion — **l'oignon (m.)**
- peas — **les petits pois**
- potato — **la pomme de terre**
- pumpkin — **la citrouille**
- spinach — **l'épinard (m.)**
- zucchini — **la courgette**

NOTES

Desserts = **Les Desserts**
Drinks = **Les Boissons**
Fish = **Le Poisson**
Fruits = **Les Fruits**
Meal = **Le Repas**
Meat = **La Viande**
Vegetables = **Les Légumes**

NOTES
Questions = **Les Questions**
Negatives = **Les Négatifs**

Questions

how	**comment**
how many	**combien de**
how much	**combien**
what	**quoi**
when	**quand**
where	**où**
which	**quel(s)/quelle(s)**
which one	**lequel/laquelle**
which ones	**lesquels/lesquelles**
who	**qui**
why	**pourquoi**

Negatives

never	**ne...jamais**
no more	**ne...plus**
no one	**ne...personne**
not	**ne...pas**
not at all	**ne...pas du tout**
not enough	**ne... pas assez**

127

not much	**ne...pas beaucoup**
not often	**ne...pas souvent**
not too much	**ne...pas trop**
not yet	**ne...pas encore**
nothing	**ne...rien**